The Planet Mercury Harnessing the Power of Your Communication

Wendy Rosenthal

Printed in the United States of America
Published in Hellertown, PA

978-1-958711-98-9

For more information or to place bulk orders, contact the author or the publisher at Jennifer@BrightCommunications.net.

Bright
COMMUNICATIONS

To Bob Weill: Bob's love, support and belief in infusing spirituality into business and guiding people to their greatness has given me the wings to do this work.

Also to my husband, son, family, and friends who support me through thick and thin.

Finally, to Rav Philip and Karen Berg, my spiritual teachers without whom I would have the connection to the spiritual wisdom of Kabbalah, which guides me in all I do.

STOP!

Before reading the insightful book don't you want to know what sign Mercury is in your personal chart?

Great, I knew you would. All you need to do is follow this QR code, fill in the form with your birth details, and submit. We will send your Mercury sign back as soon as possible!

Once you have the facts, enjoy the book!

Contents

Introduction

Paul J. Meyer, pioneer in self-improvement and achieving goals said, "Communication--the human connection--is the key to personal and career success. His important insight could not be more accurate. Since the dawn of time, humanity sought to communicate with each other--sometimes through grunts, other times through body language, and eventually through words. Communication shapes ideas, emotions, and intellect. Ideas through words can build up--or tear down--whole societies. As powerful as our communication abilities are, it is easy to take communication for granted. We slip into robotic verbal or written exchanges where even the most significant emotional phrases expressing the depths of our emotions can become trivialized.

The importance of assessing and elevating our communication style should not be underestimated. As Mr. Meyer stated, it is the key for our whole success. Fortunately, many disciplines provide techniques for determining our styles and tools for helping to evolve them.

Among all the valid and helpful tools out in the world, the one I have come to rely on in my life and my career helping my clients express their greatness comes from the stars. Every aspect of your personality and every wish, desire, ambition, and attribute that you have can be revealed through the position of the stars and planets at the moment of your birth. Your soul provided you with a guidebook, a map to understanding your true purpose via the astrological chart, which points to your many gifts and the challenges required to expose the best of who you are. My deep desire is to share my passion for unlocking the secrets openly hidden in one's chart with you so you can feel your greatness and have the means to actually do something to share it with the world.

Let Me Introduce Myself

My journey to Chief Pathfinder and Spiritual Business Guide started a long time ago in a galaxy far, far...oh sorry I am a Star Wars fan. It did start a long time ago in Los Angeles where I am from. Growing up in LaLa-land definitely impacted my drive and curiosity to seek more spiritual modalities while building a business career. After graduating from the University of Southern California with a business degree in Real Estate Property Development and Management in the middle of the first real estate crash in California, I was very fortunate to land a job in that industry.

I started my career in the real estate industry as a commercial property manager, learning the ropes for what it takes to build commercial properties, value them, lease them, build them out for tenants, and ultimately chase tenants that didn't pay. The part where I had to chase tenants that didn't pay probably was the most educational aspect of my time there--not so much fun, but educational. It started me on my journey of learning how to draw out information through nuanced inquiry. It also taught me how to deal with defensive, scared, embarrassed people who ultimately had to share their difficulties with someone they didn't know and who they perceived was working against them not with them. Who knew that rent collection could be so enlightening!

About the same time and propelled by dealing so often with difficult situations, I embarked on an internal journey that led me to explore the world of spirituality. I was looking for reasons why the world is the way it is and why people act the way they act. I wanted to make sense out of things in my own life, but I also wanted to understand if there was any bigger picture that I could latch onto and find my place in. More on this later.

After working in commercial property management for five years, I was recruited by a former boss to what started me on the biggest adventure of my life, both professionally and personally. I started as Business Development Manager and then became Senior Vice President of Business Development for Sony Development, a division of Sony Corporation that built urban entertainment centers, totalling nearly a billion dollars in three major cities: San Francisco, Tokyo, and Berlin. I was able to work with amazing people in the entertainment and real estate industries from Disney to Gensler architects to Portman Holdings. I negotiated more than $20 million in lease contracts, $7 million in sponsorship contracts, and $5 million in intellectual property rights agreements, and I learned how to ensure guests/customers at retail and entertainment venues had the best possible experience. I presented to CEOs of Fortune 400 companies, and I enticed technology startups to become partners. It was the best business school I could have attended where the grade I would receive depended on the deals I cut. I traveled all over the world and worked with people from many different cultures. I worked to be a student of business and how people showed up in business during this time.

Little did I know that having to balance the needs of our corporate objectives against those of our various partners would push me to where I am today. I had to see all sides. I had to ask so many questions to find the perfect balance that made the deals happen and ultimately what would make the project work for all. I had to learn to negotiate with others' needs in mind. I had to listen very carefully and then reflect back what I heard in the form of some kind of agreement that would get executed. On top of all that, I had to manage my own internal doubts about my capabilities and abilities to deliver. It was fascinating and enlightening, but also overwhelming and frightening all at the same time.

After completing the projects, I was asked by senior management to negotiate a management buyout from Sony and start Hyper Entertainment, a consulting firm advising the real estate and entertainment industries on creating engaging, profitable consumer experiences. Hyper Entertainment worked on high profile projects all over the world including the O2, Abbey Road Studios, and Battersea Power-Station in London, Ferrari World in Abu Dhabi and the Capitol Records building in Los Angeles. I lived in London for ten years, during which time we took Hyper Entertainment public on a small business stock exchange. Being a consultant solidified my hyper-inquisitive nature and elevated my skills at being able to pull out deeply embedded information from people, documents, and situations, shine a light on them, and deliver actionable, doable, profitable solutions.

As my journey continued, I wanted to sit on the other side of the table and have ownership of the strategies I created, so I took a break from consulting and became the Chief Marketing Officer of Jagex game developers for a couple of years. Leading a marketing department of forty during an acquisition by a private equity firm, while launching two new games definitely forced me to "own" it. I had to step up to manage my successes, and also my failures, to a board eager to measure their success in daily major wins instead of slow, steady growth. I was a bit shell-shocked, but I had accomplished much in my time there. I learned that everyone's idea of success is different and identified by different key performance indicators (KPIs) that are both quantitative and qualitative.

It was the qualitative ones that really got me. I always had to be ready for a new standard to be set and to be confident I could live up to it. That part was not so easy. Thankfully, I had my spiritual practice. Without that, personally I would have been crushed. Again, more on that in a minute.

A new baby and a new business opportunity for my husband brought me back to the United States. Hyper Entertainment became Absolute Certainty Inc. where I led the business to more projects in New York, Los Angeles, Moscow, and Saudi Arabia, as well as a couple of nonprofit groups.

In the past few years, in a moment of clarity mixed with desire to do more in my life, I realized that all the experiences I had set me up to do something I am passionate about: being a scaffold to support people and companies achieve their next level of greatness. And that is what I have been doing as the Chief Pathfinder of Pathfinder 1 to 1.

Pathfinder 1 to 1 is a coaching practice that works with clients at all levels and places in their careers to help them find a pathway to elevate skills, solve sticky problems, and see the world differently leading to more business and personal success. My unique selling proposition (USP) is that I infuse my sessions with spiritual concepts and practices, bridging physical objectives with metaphysical solutions and practical actions driven by intuition. I inspire my clients to see that by starting from the inside out they can take true control over what they believe are external obstacles inhibiting their ability to generate more success.

Okay, so what about the spirituality side of things? You might be thinking this was a book about astrology. What does business coaching have to do with any of the spirituality and astrology stuff?

Well, years ago I was challenged by a spiritual mentor at the Kabbalah Centre (a spiritual organization that teaches the ancient wisdom of Kabbalah, making it practical to use in everyday life for personal growth and transformation), who inspired me to see that how I was conducting myself in business was not the same as how I was conducting myself in my personal life. I was working hard on transforming old habits and belief systems in my personal life, trying to grow spiritually. But then I would go to work and all that I was learning and doing transformationally went out the window. I wasn't doing anything horrible, illegal, or immoral in business, but I wasn't using the practical tools I was learning in spirituality in my business life. Once my eyes were open to this, I started to see the negative impact of keeping my business life separate from my spiritual practice.

Why was this an important realization? Couldn't I continue in my business without making changes? I was doing well, traveling the world, and working on incredible projects. Well yes, I could, and I did for a while, but then I understood the calm and clarity I was beginning to feel in my private life was not extending into my business. I thought bringing spirituality into my business would be weird and not accepted by others.

Frankly, I thought it might stop me from being the go-getter, aggressive, successful businessperson I was. I wasn't equating spirituality with bottom-line success.

But then a few things, particularly with one client, provided an AHA moment. I was about a third of the way through a very big project under a multiple-year contract when the client shifted gears and terminated the agreement. It was unexpected, frustrating, and financially devastating to my company, particularly because we were a public traded company, and I would have to explain to the shareholders what happened. Yikes! At that moment, I had to make a choice: See the chaos and panic or let my spirituality guide me in a business situation that was difficult so I could see if what my mentor shared with me really works.

I chose to see that situation as an opportunity. It was the perfect scenario for me to test the spiritual principle that everything happens for a specific reason for me to do my soul's purpose.

Instead of suing the client for breach of contract, we agreed an amount that was fair compensation to end the contract. Instead of stressing about the people we had hired to work on the project, we worked with them to see if we could transfer them to other projects, and if not, we figured out a solution.

Believe me, the road was filled with bumps and not easy ones. But at the end of the day, we not only survived, we thrived. After that, the decision to explore raising my Spiritual IQ as it relates to my business to see the effects was a no-brainer. After consistent efforts to infuse spiritual practices and tools into my business, I saw it was not only possible but crucial to its success and continued growth. The journey then became how to use spirituality to help me to manage my cashflow, generate new business, negotiate contracts, and grow my bottom line. Yes, that is correct: One can use spirituality and spiritual tools to enhance their business for real because spirituality is better understanding the rules of the game--the *whole* game. And understanding that has real practical, bottom line impact. Starting with spirituality means beginning from the inside out. If something is happening externally, you look inside to see why you might need the situation and how it might benefit you. Or alternatively, why does this situation fill me with fear or other negative emotions.

Once I got the hang of it and saw the real world business impact, I knew this path was right for me and that I had to share it with the world through my coaching.

Now what about astrology... how does that fit in? I have been a student and passionate fan of astrology since I was a child. All the spiritual paths I explored led to the stars in one form or fashion. In fact, I realized that discussion of the stars and their meanings can be found in the Bible and other more traditional religious texts and commentaries--albeit sometimes in a more coded fashion.

Over the years, I took the time to learn about astrology as a hobby, until one day I did a chart reading for a friend for fun. She was so amazed at the information her chart was sharing with me and how I connected it to her business issues, she encouraged me to do this professionally. I was just starting my coaching business, so I dismissed the idea again until that same friend recommended that I read a chart for a person she was doing business with on the fly. We were literally in a business meeting, and I read his chart quickly and shared some things with him that he said resonated so much that it shifted what he was thinking about his business. From that, I saw in real time how much our astrological makeup can work as an effective tool and guide for how we can improve our lives and our businesses. And so, I went all in. I took some classes to hone my skills, asked the Universe for support, and off I went.

An Unlikely Pair: Business and Astrology

In the world of coaching, many, many assessment tools exist to help coaches understand their clients, using that information to guide them, show progress, and give insight to the client as to what may be limiting them. Some familiar ones include Myers-Briggs test, Gallup's CliftonStrengths, VIA Inventory of Strengths, Leader Competency Inventory, Mindvalley Assessment, Enneagrams, and Team Effectiveness Assessment. The list goes on, and all these assessments are valid, useful tools. So, what makes astrology better?

Each one of us is a multi-layered unique being made up of genetics, experiences, learned behaviors, and belief systems that shape who we are and what we do. The combination of all those influences is like DNA. Its combination is unique to you. DNA allows for scientists to make a more accurate assessment about the whole person then it would if just by knowing one gene.

In the same way, astrology allows one to see a fuller, more three-dimensional picture of a person than what you might see if you were using one of the business assessment tools, without having to coordinate and connect several assessments to see the bigger picture. Astrology also reveals the intricate connections between differing aspects of a person's attributes much more easily because it is all there in one place. One can see the link between how someone might deal with stress and the partners they attract in their life. Or a connection can be made between how someone deals with emotions and the belief systems they are likely to create.

To make an analogy, astrology compared with a personality test is the difference between seeing a fetus on a sonogram or on a 3D scan that shows the face of an unborn child. The depth of information is quite astonishing even in its most basic form, at the natal chart, the chart developed from the moment of one's birth and focusing on where the planets and astrological signs intersect.

A person's astrological DNA indicates how they will engage in their personal life, and it also suggests how they will carry that into their career, relationships at work, communication, and financial acumen or lack thereof and also how they manifest things in their life, how they overcome obstacles, and how they level up throughout their lives. In my mind, astrology is the *best* business assessment tool around. In ninety minutes, I can see a picture of my client that helps me help them in a deeper way.

Not every client wants a chart reading, and that is perfectly acceptable. I can draw out the same information over time by getting to know them, but an astrological chart condenses time for them and for me. A client's chart helps me quickly see the areas to focus my attention. For example, certain signs are really adept at generating money but are less able to engage one-to-one with others. If the person with that sign is looking to be in a management role because their company thinks they will help them generate more money that way, I can quickly give them guidance on how to manage their team in a style that will better suit them and get the best out of their team.

I know many people in the world do not connect with astrology. They look at it as a dark art, not based in science, or an airy-fairy carnival trick because it is seen as a prognostication tool. And that is fair. I do not require any of my clients to have a chart reading because I am a big believer in resonance. If a certain practice or modality doesn't resonate with you, you should not force yourself to do it.

Also on many levels, I can agree with some of the criticisms on how astrology is used or misused. For example, I would not use astrology as a main tool to determine what stocks I should buy, nor which company would be a solid investment. What I say to clients who are not interested in chart reading is after having read hundreds of charts there is valuable information in it, and if one is willing, it is worth at least hearing about themselves from a different perspective.

Astrology: The Map of the Soul

The Oxford Dictionary describes astrology as the "study of the movements and relative positions of celestial bodies interpreted as having an influence on human affairs and the natural world." That's pretty straightforward, but it leaves so much on the table.

Your astrological identity, which is expressed for us to see through your astrological chart, is truly the map of your soul. I hope I am blowing your mind a little bit because there is so much wrapped up in saying the "map of the soul." First, you need to consider that the soul exists and that it can be mapped. Then you might ask yourself why would you need a map of the soul? If I have a soul, then wouldn't I know about it? It is mine after all! Raising and answering those questions alone can be the basis for a very long workshop, lecture, debate, and discussion. Because this book is not specifically about the soul, I will not dive deeply into it, but I do want to address it because it provides context for my view of astrology being the map of the soul.

My understanding of the soul comes from more than a few spiritual modalities. Despite their differing origins, most of their explanations will intersect many times, validating the universal truth of the soul and its journey. However, one spiritual modality, the Kabbalah, explains the soul and its journey in a clear, comprehensible way so it is the one I lean on the most to explain it for the purposes of making the connection to astrology.

So here is the very, very, very consolidated version of the Story of Creation. Each one of us has a soul that is but a small piece of a unified soul that the Creative Force of the Universe (God, Allah, Buddha, Source, or whatever your idea of a Creator is) created in order to share its pure, giving light with no limitations. As this unified soul received this endless light, it realized it wanted to be like its creator and share as well. Because there was no one for this soul to share with as the Creative Force of the Universe did not need anything for it is all things and it wanted to give the unified soul what it wanted, it created our world and shattered the one soul into many so we would ultimately be able to practice our desire to share with others. Even though the soul was essentially shattered into smaller "pieces" (and continues to be), there is a universal connectivity between each of us as well as soul groups that tend to travel through lifetimes together in order to help each other achieve their individual purpose.

Each individual soul was imbued with its own greatness (including some not-so-great traits), which allows it to grow, expand, and ultimately become closer and closer to the source as humanity as a whole moves toward a more peaceful time. Each soul can come into the world multiple times to do its work or purpose. If it doesn't get it right the first time, it can choose to come back. There are many reasons and benefits to trying to play the game again if it doesn't succeed, which is why souls do opt in. "Opting in" means being constricted to the body and the heaviness of that as well as the entirety of each of our souls is much more expansive than what can actually be held by the body consciousness. So the soul has to have a good reason for jumping back in.

What are some of the reasons for the soul to come back? Here is a list of the few I have read about across all modalities.

- The soul saw what it could have done better in one area and wants to correct a specific action, event, or attribute.
- The soul wants to help a specific soul or group of souls.
- The soul has one task it has to finish to go to its next level in the metaphysical world.
- The soul might have left this world before its time and did not get to finish its work in general.
- The soul wants to help the world as a whole move closer to a time of overall peace.
- The soul has a particular attribute that the world needs, and it is asked to rejoin the human race.

Once the soul decides to adorn a new body, it has new choices to make. It knows the work it has to do, the tools it will need to do that work, and that once it arrives on the earthly plane, it will not be able to clearly communicate with the body consciousness to share what it knows. It is for this reason that the soul is very careful in choosing the place, time, date, and family/situation into which it will be born. The family part is often connected with the grouping of souls it has been connected with over lifetimes, but often the roles are changed. What was the father is now the brother, for example.

The family situation is a tool because it is the most direct, intense way to see the karmic debt we all have to pay. No one pushes our buttons or elevates us the way our family does! The rest of the tools we need are those attributes both good and bad, expansive and limiting, painful and pain-free. These attributes make us, us. Part of our purpose during our life is to use our gifts to elevate our limited selves and use our limited selves as a way to let our greatness shine through our gifts. It is a beautiful cycle of transformation and growth. And as we grow, we shine our unique light into the world, creating a ripple effect that we cannot even conceive of. Likewise, when we get bogged down in our limited selves, we take away from the overall process of the world.

I am not saying this to make anyone feel badly or negative. None of us are perfect, nor are we meant to be. At its most basic level, the work of our soul is to let more of our amazing light shine, regardless of the challenges that might present to us. We want to operate at a higher vibration so the world can as well. That is part of the rules of life...free will. To really do the work of our soul, we must make the choices along the way that either elevate us or keep us at the level we are.

Because the voice of our soul is relatively quiet and difficult for us to focus on, ways have been created to allow us to amplify the volume. Meditation, sound baths, energy work, and even tarot cards allow our souls' voices to be heard. All are valid, but for me, they are less accessible than understanding your astrological makeup. Astrology is the most direct way to understand the selection of tools your soul chose for you to navigate through the journey of life. When you understand that better, you understand you better.

Astrology, Religion, and Other Spiritual Modalities

The use of astrology definitely generates copious commentary from across the religious, spiritual, and even political spectrum. As I mentioned before, people can view it as a dark art or airy-fairy, having no value beyond a fun parlor trick. If I had not become a practitioner myself, I might be swayed by the thought that astrology is just a fun hobby best left to the interest pages of a newspaper or astrology website.

But as I took my journey to discover the depths of it as a practice, I discovered that astrology has its roots in the ancient world and the beginning of humanity, plus many religious and spiritual modalities use astrology even if it doesn't seem obvious or that it is overtly accepted but base many of its traditions and writings on it. On top of that, astrology is amazingly accurate as I have found in the reactions from clients I have never met, reflecting that I nailed their makeup spot on.

Exploration of some of these connections and uses is worth a minor diversion in this book not for me to convince you of anything, but to hopefully inspire your own investigation into the use and validity of the practice.

The Bible: Old and New Testaments

In general, the ancient world relied on the sky to guide them in many ways as a daily practice. Although some people regarded it as going against the Divine, it was acknowledged that even Jesus spoke about astrology and the influence of the stars.

Many citations of the sun, moon, and stars and their effects on humanity and the planet are referenced throughout both the Old and New Testaments. Some are overt, for example, the use of stars to navigate, as in the case of the Star of Bethlehem leading the Wise Men to the birth of Jesus. Others are more concealed, as is the discussion about celebrating the New

Moon in the Old Testament. It takes deeper study in the Talmud and other commentaries about the Old Testament regarding the New Moon to gain further information on the importance of the New Moon to humanity.

Another example of a more esoteric interpretation of the mention of astrology can be found in commentaries about the Old Testament cites that the twelve tribes are actually representative of the twelve signs of the Zodiac. When the tribes are mentioned in the Torah, it is actually an indication that we have the power to evolve and overcome the less positive aspects of our nature as understood in astrology and represented by the tribes.

As the world evolved and religion became more of a way to control behavior, astrology was often compared to the "Devil's Work" or associated with magic or wizardry. It started to lose its connection as a powerful way to view our world.

Sefer Yetzirah

The Sefer Yetzirah (The Book of Formation) is an ancient book of mysticism that is believed by most to have been written by Abraham, the Patriarch, himself. It is an esoteric manuscript that provides insight to the creation of the Universe, as well as how the constellations were created and their purpose.

There is a manuscript of The Sefer Yetzirah in the British Museum, and many scholars both of Jewish background and from other religions have worked to understand the depth of it. The Kabbalah discusses the connection of this book to astrology through the use of gematria ("a Kabbalistic method of interpreting the Hebrew scriptures by computing the numerical value of words, based on those of their constituent letters".[1]) where it is able to identify the discussion of the individual signs and what nature in people is represented.

Eastern Religions

Chinese Astrology, which has its foundation in Taoism and then later practiced in the Buddhist religion, connects the Zodiac very clearly with the way a person behaves. And while the signs are more described as animals and not the constellations themselves, there are many, many touchpoints that reflect the same descriptions of one's nature. Eastern religions as in the West used and still use astrology to predict societal events in general and personally.

Islam

While there is debate about allowing the use of astrology in Islam, its use dates back centuries with nobles and caliphs employing astrologers to help guide them during times of peace and war and for business. There was an acceptance of astrology because it took a more scientific approach, stemming from the practice of astronomy. Zodiac symbols were adopted in art and literature. There were even doctors in the Islamic world who relied heavily on astrology to help their patients.

The Zohar

The Zohar is the foundational text of the Kabbalah and is a coded and extremely esoteric explanation of the Old Testament. Conveyed by Rabbi Shimon bar Yochai in the second century CE to a group of nine friends, the Zohar is said to include revelations about the formation of the Universe, human nature, and man's connection to the Creator. The Zohar is many volumes long and has several sets of books that address different topics.

The Zohar speaks extensively about astrology and the impact of the stars on humanity as well as its connection to the Old Testament as it deciphers the deeper meaning of the scripture.

Much of what I learned personally about astrology stems from my study of Kabbalah and the Zohar, along with more traditional forms of study. I focused on this practice because I like to understand the why of things not just the how. The Zohar (and those who now interpret it) provide me with much more insight that I take into my reading of astrological charts.

What's in a Chart?

There is so much to share about how a simple astrological chart communicates the entirety of you. And quite frankly, that is not the purpose of this book. However, it is useful to provide you with some context and understanding about what is the makeup of the signs, planets, and the chart. It is like Astrology Pre-101.

The chart is a two-dimensional expression of what is a vast, three-dimensional (actually probably even four) expanse called our Universe. It seeks to capture simply the movement of the planets and constellations through time and across distances. The chart represents all this information from our vantage point, meaning the perspective is from a point on Earth as if it is at the center of the Universe, not the sun.

Because astrological charts are represented in two dimensions as 360-degree circle, layers of information can be expressed on it. From the basic Zodiac signs, the twelve houses, the intersection of the planet and signs at the moment of birth, the various aspects between the planets at the moment of birth to the degree the planet was in each sign at the moment of birth, you can find it all in the circle. And that is not an exhaustive list of what can be found in an astrological chart! Your soul has so many things to share with you through the tool of astrology.

The chart's circle is divided into twelve sections of the circle of 30 degrees each. Each section is identified by a sign of the Zodiac as well as representing an astrological house, which will be explained. We will delve a little deeper into each sign as we explore how the Planet Mercury impacts them, but here is a list of the signs and the dates they are activated. Please note the astrological year begins with the sign of Aries in the month of March.

Aries	March 21 - April 20
Taurus	April 21 - May 20
Gemini	May 21 - June 20
Cancer	June 21 - July 20
Leo	July 21 - August 20
Virgo	August 21 - September 20
Libra	September 21 - October 20
Scorpio	October 21 - November 20
Sagittarius	November 21 - December 20
Capricorn	December 21 - January 20
Aquarius	January 21 - February 20
Pisces	February 21 - March 20

The table represents the answer to that famous question, "What sign are you?" and it reflects how we determine our Sun Sign. Anyone reading this book probably knows what their Sun Sign is, and if you do not, you can go to any newspaper or magazine, open it up to the astrology feature, and find out. While your Sun Sign is important, you will very quickly come to understand it is a small part of who we are.

The planets and stars move through the universe, crossing paths and lining up in various configurations, expressing different aspects of the soul and the tools it brings with it into this world.

The intersection between the planets and the stars is where I focus because those points reflect the unique combination of our strengths and weaknesses and how they interact to help us transform and improve in various situations of our life.

Before diving into how the signs are organized, I want to touch on some important elements of the chart that are not signs or planets. They add to the depth of wisdom that can be attained through it.

The Twelve Houses

Each 30-degree section of the chart represents one of the Twelve Houses of the Zodiac. Each house covers a different aspect of life and is connected to a major attribute of the sign with which it shares a section. Understanding the House in which a planet and sign intersect provides a sharp focus on certain areas of your life. For example, if you are having relationship problems, it is helpful to look at the seventh house, what planet in what sign is there, so you can hone in on how you would approach the problem given your astrological makeup and what solutions you can use to overcome them. The following shows what the Twelve Houses are and what each represents.

House	Attribute	Zodiac Sign
First House	The Self	Aries
Second House	Money, Prosperity, Possessions	Taurus
Third House	Communication/ Education	Gemini
Fourth House	Family/Home	Cancer
Fifth House	Pleasure/ Entertainment	Leo
Sixth House	Health	Virgo
Seventh House	Relationships	Libra
Eighth House	Transformation	Scorpio
Ninth House	Purpose	Sagittarius
Tenth House	Career	Capricorn
Eleventh House	Social Life	Aquarius
Twelfth House	Spirituality	Pisces

Many times, there are no signs in a house, which indicates a neutral area of your life, one neither challenging nor an area of greatness.

The Lunar Nodes

The Lunar Nodes are geographic points at which the moon's orbit crosses the Earth's ecliptic or orbital plane. The orbital plane is the path the Earth takes around the Sun. There is a North Node and a South Node. The North Node represents a person's Karmic debt, and the South Node gives insight to a person's past life. Comprehending the Lunar Nodes help build the picture of some of the challenges faced and how to repair them in this life.

Aspects

As the planets and stars move through the universe on their individual paths or orbits, the influence they have on each other is visualized by the position of one in terms of degrees to the other at any given moment. Aspects are always changing because the universe is always moving. While an aspect can last for years because of the distance of the objects, other aspects can change throughout the day.

Aspects help us understand relationships to ourselves, our work, and to people around us. Five major aspects exist, each defining the type of relationship we have around the attributes that the planet represents within the backdrop of the Zodiac sign.

Aspect	Position	Influence
Conjunction	At or close to the same degree	The energy represented by each planet is aligned and therefore amplified in the person's life. It is generally favorable, although it can lead to a blind spot for the person in that area.

Aspect	Position	Influence
Sextile	60 degrees apart	The energies are working together harmoniously and give you a heightened talent in that area or ability to cultivate talent more than one's own natural ability.
Square	90 degrees apart	This is a clash of energy, which can be very uncomfortable. The planets involved are competitive, which can lead to internal frustration, conflict, and a feeling of working at cross purposes.
Trine	120 degrees apart	Trines are an alignment of the same energy, which is favorable and natural. A trine is like a basic sugar cookie. It is good but nothing special.
Opposition	180 degrees apart	The energy mirrors the name in that this aspect can be very challenging. It is an energy of extremes, pushing a person from one extreme or another and back again. An opposition of two planets can also foster uncertainty.

In order to provide you an idea of how all of these elements line up in a chart, I have shared my personal basic natal chart, featuring the signs, houses, and aspects. Again, this is a simple chart, not encompassing all the elements available to display. Even at its most basic, it is clear from the combinations of information that can be garnered through the chart that it is abundant. For example, if one reads only the planets and signs in one house, rich data could be cultivated.

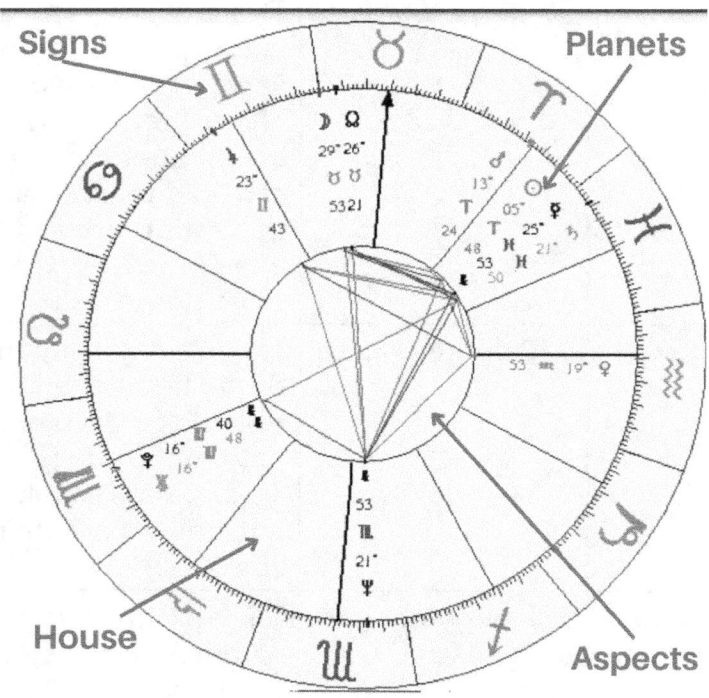

The highlighted areas show the key elements outlined so you can see the layers of information contained in a chart. Symbols for planets and signs create a shorthand, allowing for more information to be included. Many websites offer free charts like this one, if you are interested in running your chart specifically so you can see the map of your soul.

Many permutations of a natal chart exist to gain specific information.

- Progression charts move your natal chart along in time to any particular day, including in the future, which lets you see growth as well as allows for future insight and predictions.
- Location charts provide insight into what cities and countries might support your soul's journey in the best manner.
- A focused chart might reveal a path to love, career, or prosperity.
- Some charts can hone in on past lives and karma.
- You can even have a comparison chart to see how two lives intersect and overlap.

This is why one can have their chart read more than one time. There is so much to learn and so many different lenses through which your attributes are elicited, the usefulness of multiple chart reading becomes apparent. It is also worth reiterating here no one piece of an astrological chart can be taken in isolation entirely. I say this even though this book is looking at one aspect of our chart, the Planet Mercury and how that impacts communication. As I mentioned previously, the whole chart is like looking at DNA, while looking at one's Sun Sign, Mercury Sign, etc. is akin to understanding in detail only the gene that reflects one's eye color. One's Sun Sign does impact one's Mercury sign, which is why doing a full chart reading will always provide much deeper insight.

This point does not negate the value of focusing on individual planets and their influence because there is value in knowing the general way the influence works in our life...if nothing else to help us grow just a little bit!

My talent when reading a chart lies in extracting one's gifts and challenges and connecting the dots on how to optimize the gifts and utilize the challenges in a more effective way. What I might see in a chart can be extremely different than what another would, and that is good. My charts are great at spotlighting key attributes and providing transformative actions as a result of what is seen. As I said before, this is very practical.

The Planets and Their Meanings

With a view to the sky instead of a chart-filled paper, it is time to turn our attention to the meaning of the planets. Each known planet (and even some small asteroids) whose orbits take them around our Sun have been observed and mapped over the course of history dating to early civilizations. As technology and science improved over time, planets, asteroids, and stars have been added into the mix or in some cases reduced to a minor influence.

The planets capturing the most attention in the basic charts for the longest time historically are the Sun, Moon, Mercury, Venus, Mars, Jupiter, and Saturn. The focus evolved because these celestial bodies were the most visible given the technology of the time. For the most part, they still make up the bulk of what astrologers explore today, but Uranus, Neptune, Pluto, and Chiron (a small asteroid) are now permanently nestled into modern day charts, even with Pluto's demotion to a dwarf planet.

The historical astrological attributes assigned to the planets echo or perhaps were created as a result of the stories from Roman and Greek mythology. More than a few mythological characters are connected to the heavens and are in our lexicon today. The names of our planets are mythological characters and hint at the attributes they represent.

Astrologers employ the attributes of each planet in the chart to guide their interpretation. For example, one aspect of the planet Mars is connected with taking action. The astrologer will see what sign Mars was in at the time of birth and that will illuminate how a person takes action. The layers of attributes of a planet aid in interpreting the layers of each one of us.

A key point to make is the newly discovered planets of Uranus, Neptune, and Pluto and Chiron point to generational attributes in a person, meaning the specific influence created by the Zodiac present at the time of one's birth affect all those born in a generational span in the same way as a result of the length of time it take for these planets to rotate around the sun. They also represent the more mystical side of our personalities indicative of their mysterious natures produced by distance from Earth. For example, a generational group can be more spiritual, revolutionary, or practical. These planets provide a more communal context for choices we make instead of more personal ones. Do not get me wrong, the influence is definitely significant as your soul chose the time of birth and needs to be in a certain generation to do its transformational work. However, regardless of the personal changes you make, these influences will be running in the background.

Let's dive into the planet's driving attributes that impact our lives.

The Sun

The Sun represents that part of ourselves that we illuminate to the rest of the world. These attributes are most familiar to our friends, family, coworkers, and ourselves. It is the part of ourselves that we take for granted or the areas of our personality that we say, "I was just born this way." For example, if you are a natural hard worker or naturally friendly. It is how you see yourself. Our Sun Sign is the easiest to calculate because we just need to know our birthdays. It is what you read in an astrological report that you find online or in a newspaper. The Sun represents our surface and default personality. And while our Sun Sign is important to our astrological makeup, it is not as significant as the world of astrology makes it out to be. I feel this is why so often people in one breath might comment that you are so like your Sun Sign, yet in the next breath they might say an action of yours seems unlike what a typical (insert sign here) does.

I believe if you want to transform an area of your personality or internal attribute, the traits of the Sun Sign is the best place to start.

The Rising (Ascendant) Sign

While not a planet, the rising sign is another geographical point extremely relevant in contributing to your astrological makeup. Calculated as the sign that was rising on the eastern horizon at the point of your birth, the rising sign represents a deeper internal, less showy part of your nature. In many ways, your true personality, the one that only you share with others when you feel safe and less vulnerable, is represented by the Rising Sign.

The Rising Sign can be less familiar to us. I like to think of it as those parts of me that I wonder where that part of me came from. Our Rising Sign is like the power tool in our tool box. We can rely on this part of ourselves when we need to take ourselves to our next level.

I believe the Rising Sign is our driving force that can propel us to new heights if we learn how to capture and embrace its significance in our lives.

The Moon Sign

Like the Moon profoundly affects the tides of the Earth's oceans, the Moon rules our emotions. Our Moon Sign explains how we deal with emotional triggers especially when we are at our most raw and reactive. It indicates how we might "come out swinging" if pushed to our limits emotionally. The Moon Sign also represents our connection to our mothers as well as how one might behave as a mother.

The Planet Venus

The Planet Venus embodies the way in which we approach and behave in our relationships: family, friends, spouses, children, lovers, partners, and customers included. Our lives are intertwined with so many others, some with glorious effects and others with disastrous ones. Understanding the lens through which we engage with people on a surface level as well in more intimate situations can be life-changing.

Likewise, Venus also reveals the direction our creative and aesthetic nature takes and can speak to how we design our homes, our artistic ability, and our thought process when approaching situations that require us to think in new ways.

The Planet Mars

The planet of war is also the planet of action and desire. Mars represents the process we see represented all around us from the beginning of a thought through to its manifestation, including the inevitable stumbling blocks we might encounter along the way.

Mars kicks off the way we engage in any process by providing clarity about how we activate our desire for something. Do we crave or just wish for things to happen? Next Mars sets out how we take action to achieve our desires. Are we methodical, do we rush to do something, or are we happy to sit back and let things evolve around us? Mars then shines a light on how we deal with confrontations and obstacles that happen along the way. It helps understand our fight, flight, freeze reaction in a new light.

The Planet Jupiter

The largest planet in our solar system, it seems only right that it shines a light on our personal, growth, expansion, and access to blessings. Jupiter points us in the direction to the place beyond our comfort zone, to the place where we surpass our fears and align with our soul's purpose.

Jupiter helps us to understand where our hidden gifts reside and how to empower them to achieve more than we believe that we can.

The Planet Saturn

For as expansive as Jupiter is, Saturn is equally limiting. Saturn is often called the "policeman" of the universe because it will quickly slap your hand metaphorically when we venture into repetitive behaviors. Saturn is the expression of what our limited belief systems are and how they stop us from our true purpose in this life.

Even though it seems as if Saturn is highlighting negativity in our lives, I believe it is one of the most useful planets in terms of driving us to transform because it clearly defines the aspects of our internal self that need the most attention. Saturn is like the mirror in Snow White that tells us we are not what we think we are--sometimes in a very direct way. While not always easy to hear, Saturn plays the role for our benefit.

The Planet Uranus

Uranus physically is tilted at such a steep degree that it looks like it is orbiting the sun on its side, which falls in line with the traits it conveys. Rebellion, eccentricity, and upheaval characterize this unique planet. As mentioned earlier, Uranus is a generational planet, one that influences millions of people globally. So how the generation reacts to world events is guided by this energy and can often be felt worldwide.

The Planet Neptune

Dreamy, spiritual, and magical best describe the nature of Neptune and the influence it has over us. Neptune pushes us internally and asks us to think beyond the realm of our five senses. It allows us to believe we can break free from the material world and pushes us to explore the possibilities that our limitless soul can help guide us in our day lives. When you see eras of rapid invention or exploration, Neptune has been activated. Neptune also encourages us to be more compassionate and supportive of others.

The Planet Pluto

At the edge of our solar system, Pluto receives the least amount of energy from our Sun, and fittingly its energy and influence are connected to transformation, destruction, and death. Sounds ominous! However, these forces are part of life and do not always indicate something negative. Pluto inspires us to let go of the past and things that do not serve us. Pluto reminds us that we sometimes have to tear down to rebuild better. It supports our efforts to transform areas of our lives that we want to improve upon.

Building the Zodiac: Elements and Modalities

With the understanding of what the planets represent, it's time to share a quick overview of how the Zodiac signs are structured and categorized. Each layer of information acts as a guide for understanding the map of your soul.

Elements

Each sign is connected to one of the four elements: fire, earth, air, and water. The elements determine the energy of the sign. Each sign has an external element and an internal element associated with the sign. The external element relates the energy we exude outwardly, and the internal element is connected to our internal emotions and how we tend to internalize the world around us.

Fire Signs (Aries, Leo, Sagittarius) ignite energy, thoughts, and actions wherever they go. They love to start things but struggle to finish. They can burn out quickly. They also have a deep well of energy and are the first ones to jump into action when needed and even when it is not, which can sometimes have a negative result. They can be very explosive and quick to anger but again what started as an explosion often fizzles out quickly. If a Fire Sign is angry at you, let them yell for a bit without response, and they are likely to calm down quickly. Fuel their flames, and you might be in it for a while!

They shine very bright, and they know it and love it, enjoying center stage as often as possible. Their luminous energy attracts people from near and far. Fire Signs usually have lots of "followers," people who like to be around their energy, literally basking in their sunlight. And Fire Signs give very freely as well so that keeps their "groupies" engaged!

Fire Signs like to move, and action is their native language. You will not see a Fire Sign sitting around for too long. If you want to start something but do not know how, find a Fire Sign, and they will set you on the right path. Fire Signs tend to attract prosperity, but they struggle to keep money because they like to spend and be generous with it.

Earth Signs (Taurus, Virgo, Capricorn) are the stable signs of the group. Not quick to react nor take action, Earth Signs like to take their time in moving one way or the other. They are methodical and will map out a path of action before taking a step towards that action. Sometimes the planning takes more time than the actual doing! Building momentum is key for an Earth Sign because inertia plays a big role in their lives. Change can happen, but it will not be quick if they have to instigate it. If they are forced to change, they seek to minimize the effect of what the changes must be.

Earth Signs are very connected to nature and feel energized by being in nature. It is very important for Earth Signs to be able to connect the world around them frequently to keep their energy up and moving. Earth Signs love beauty and seek it out wherever they can. Earth Signs are very loyal, and their friends and family appreciate this aspect tremendously, often going to them for support and advice.

Earth Signs have deep emotions but do not often put them on display. They take their time in processing emotions, but once they feel comfortable with someone, they are very loving, generous, and supportive. Earth Signs are very good with money because they are good at earning it, keeping it, and figuring it out how to make it grow. However, they can become too attached to the material world and what money brings, which can turn their focus away from their interpersonal activities and their internal growth.

Air Signs (Gemini, Libra, Aquarius) are like a warm breeze. They are light, warm, refreshing, and temporary. Air Signs lean toward moving from one thing to another from one minute to the next. They are hard to keep up with physically and mentally. They love learning and knowledge and will spend a little bit of time learning about a lot of things. They are usually very smart, and so they will turn that little bit of learning into a font of knowledge, even if some of it is created out of thin air. They exemplify the saying "Jack of all trades, master of none."

Air Signs are great communicators and persuaders. Verbal gymnastics are a favorite sport, so trying to outwit them in a debate might be difficult. Logic plays a big part in how they learn and deliver their thoughts about anything. Boredom with topics, jobs, people, you name it, is a challenge for an Air Sign, so finishing projects or staying in long-term relationships can be a bit unnatural and therefore hard to elicit from them.

Known for their airy personality, Air Signs are a pleasure to be around. Humor comes easy to them, much to the delight of their friends and family. Like Fire Signs, they draw a large crowd into their circle. But don't ask an Air Sign for deep emotional bonding. That is very out of their comfort zone and not likely to happen without prompting. They live in the brain, not the heart. Because of their intelligence, they are good at making money and need lessons in how to save for the future!

Water Signs (Cancer, Scorpio, Pisces) ebb and flow like the waves of the ocean. Their emotions rule, and they are incredibly intuitive, sometimes connecting more with the unseen world then they let on. Sensitive to a fault, Water Signs' emotions can be triggered easily, and the expression of their emotions often seep out days, months, or years beyond the initial trigger. Because they are ruled by water, they tend to think non-linearly, so their journey to a conclusion can be unorthodox or difficult for others to understand. They do get there in the end, but it might be a bit of a trek. Empathy reigns in the world of the Water Signs, feeling the emotions of others sometimes as much as they feel their own, which can give them a leg up in terms of assessing people and situations. As long as they do not lose themselves in others' emotions or assume they fully know what the other is thinking, they can really change people's lives by connecting on that emotional level.

Water Signs face self-destructive tendencies because their emotions can take them over to a point where they do not feel they can find a way to overcome something difficult. Staying away from artificial ways like drugs or alcohol to lighten their emotional load actually helps them stay off that path. Water

Signs create naturally, and you find many artists, writers, performers, designers, and actors are one of the Water Signs, or Water Signs feature predominantly in their chart. An angst that Water Signs possess is expressed in elevated ways through the arts.

Water Signs love being in relationships and are typically loving and supportive. They can go overboard on occasion and stay in relationships too long or believe there is more to the relationship when there is nothing there. Water Signs tend to focus on a few close relationships rather than having a bevy of friends. They generate money easily as well as keeping it as they have a penchant for feeling safe and secure. If they are not feeling safe and secure however, they can waste money on things or activities that provide little long-term financial stability.

The following chart outlines the signs and both their external and internal elements. You will notice that sometimes the external and internal elements are seemingly contradictory. Maybe a Fire Sign has an internal element of water. This does not mean the person who is that sign is confused, it just means they have an extra tool that helps them do their transformational work. And likewise, if a person has an external and internal element that are the same, it points to a person who's transformational work in those areas is more pronounced and focused.

Zodiac Sign	External Element	Internal Element
Aries	Fire	Water
Taurus	Earth	Fire
Gemini	Air	Air
Cancer	Water	Water
Leo	Fire	Fire
Virgo	Earth	Air
Libra	Air	Water
Scorpio	Water	Fire

Zodiac Sign	External Element	Internal Element
Sagittarius	Fire	Air
Capricorn	Earth	Water
Aquarius	Air	Fire
Pisces	Water	Air

Modalities

Three modalities exist in astrology, indicating the primary manner in which a particular sign operates when moving through their daily life. The three modalities are cardinal, fixed, and mutable. Each element contributes one sign to each of the three modalities.

The following lists the modalities and the signs associated with them.

Modalities	Signs
Cardinal	Aries, Cancer, Libra, Capricorn
Fixed	Taurus, Leo, Scorpio, Aquarius
Mutable	Gemini, Virgo, Sagittarius, Pisces

Cardinal Signs instigate by nature. They tend to be at the front end of a process and enjoy the thrill of figuring things out and getting things launched. Leadership is one of their stronger qualities, and you will see them jumping in first as a rule. They do not have to be pushed into anything, and in fact they are great at convincing others to come along. Finishing something is their weakness however, and learning to give space for other ideas comes with practice, not naturally.

Fixed Signs count stamina as one of their main characteristics. They are the engine that takes things from start to finish. Reliability and loyalty play a huge factor in their makeup, allowing them to bring the best resources to the table on every level. And you never can count a Fixed Sign out because they embody persistence and fortitude. On the more challenging side, stubbornness seeps from every pore of a Fixed Sign's body. Once they see a way to go, moving them to another path, even a better path, might feel very challenging. Lead with the benefits for the change, and you will start to get somewhere.

Mutable Signs embrace change and transitions, preparing for what is next, which they can do on more than one thing all at one time. Multitasking is their passion and going with the flow is their mantra. Intellectual and wise, Mutable Signs know things in life are always moving, changing, and evolving, so nothing seems to really bother them for too long. The flipside for them is focus. Pinning them down presents challenges for themselves and others as they try to work too much into their full lives.

The Planet Mercury: Ruler of Communication

With your understanding of basic astrology expanded, now is the time to feed your desire to learn how to enhance your communication skills and learn a little bit about how the Planet Mercury can assist you to better understand your career choices and learning style. That is right: The Planet Mercury opens the path of understanding in general, how we communicate, where we communicate it, and what is the best way for us to learn about what we want to communicate.

The fastest planet to orbit our Sun, Mercury infuses urgency into all we do and the clarity with which we do it. Mercury is all about thought processes and how those thoughts get expressed into our world. The Planet Mercury demands that we see all the possibilities that are available and quickly synthesize to form opinions and take action. Brooding or stewing in emotions is not tolerated in the world of Mercury, which points to positive and negative outcomes.

Generally, Mercury has great energy to help us be successfully proactive, especially when you understand which sign Mercury was in at the time of your birth.

Scientists, doctors, and psychologists have studied communication from the dawn of time. It has even been noted that single cell life forms develop ways to communicate with one another. From animals to humans, very little in the world would manifest if it were not for our ability to communicate with each other and even across species.

Even when the challenge to communicate seems insurmountable as in the case of Helen Keller, who could not see nor hear, she found a way to communicate, using signs formed in the hands of her teacher. Communication is a natural imperative that does not require a formal language. Signs, signals, pictures, cave drawings, symbols, and body language all provide ways for us to communicate with one another without speaking.

Communication is vital in everything from our personal relationships to our work, even the words we use internally so how we communicate to ourselves is equally vital. Communication underlies everything we do every day. Deeply understanding what drives our communication and looking at the areas where we can improve how we process what we want to say and how to say it can take us to the next level of our greatness, because communication infiltrates every aspect of our lives, every day of our lives. When we communicate at a higher level, everything else levels up, our careers, our relationships and our ability to impact the world around us.

Not only is the Planet Mercury connected to how we communicate and learn, it plays an active role in business, careers, and in today's world technology. Like the Moon moves our emotions as it waxes and wanes during the month, Mercury can wreak havoc on our lives when it turns retrograde. If you have not heard about the three week span of time that generally happens four times a year known as Mercury in Retrograde, you probably have felt its effects. When a planet is in "retrograde" it appears that it is moving backwards across our sky from our point of view. Planets do not actually move backward...it is an optical illusion caused by the different orbits the planets take around the sun. However, what being in retrograde means astrologically is a reversal of nature of the planet.

If Mercury signifies swift, urgent action and direct communication, Mercury is Retrograde effectuates a slowdown in everything we do, adding garbled communication in just for fun! When Mercury is in retrograde, we struggle to speak clearly, and miscommunication becomes the norm, verbally, in writing, and technologically. Computers break down, emails are sent to the wrong person, the internet slows down unexpectedly, and fights between calm and loving people can become the new norm at least temporarily.

Mercury in Retrograde definitely amplifies the limitless value good communication offers us!

Aries

As the first sign of the Zodiac, Aries approaches everything with a child's energy, like they are seeing something for the first time every time. They love anything new. Aries jump into any situation without thought as they love to be first. "Early adopters" describes the Aries energy perfectly. A Fire Sign, Aries attract people because of their fun, energetic, childlike nature. Seeing an Aries at the center of a crowd rates as normal in their world for many reasons, the least of which being the center of anything is right where they want to be. Attention seeking does not thrill them, but if the situation arises, they will not pass up the opportunity to draw the spotlight to themselves.

Natural born leaders, the Aries happily pave the way and encourage people to follow them, which can be hard to resist because their confidence in what they are doing and how they are doing it provides a sense of security and confidence in others. And once an Aries generates a plan, they stick to it almost to the exclusion of accepting that other ways exist to achieve the same objective. They truly love to be right and will waste time proving it to anyone who will listen...not one of their most endearing attributes!

Aries are inclined to focus their attention on themselves. "It's all about me" passes through an Aries's mind unintentionally or intentionally often during the day. Caring about others has importance to them, but their needs will take precedence.

My favorite analogy centers on a buffet table at a dinner. The Aries will be the first in line even if they have to push in front of someone to get there to make sure they have access to everything they want to put on their plate. Once they have their plate set and at the table, they will enthusiastically offer to get anyone else what they need. They will even stand in line again for another person as long as their plate is waiting for them.

Aries struggle to finish what they start because their comfort comes in experiencing and starting new things. Creativity abounds because they approach everything as if they had not seen it before, so they do not get stuck in old thought processes. Sharing their ideas is one of their favorite pastimes because they think their ideas are amazing and right and also because they enjoy sparking others to ride along with them.

Like a good Fire Sign, they are quick to anger and might explode like dynamite if someone pushes the wrong button. The explosion can cause a lot of damage to those in the way of it, but Aries are equally quick to move past an incident and even forget it moments later. And because their internal element is water, they will feel the pain their explosion caused and try to repair the damage. If an explosion of anger comes their way, they quickly brush it off and really have no memory of past deeds done to them and almost do not know how to hold a grudge.

Mercury in Aries

A person whose Mercury is in Aries will enjoy talking a lot and often about themselves and their adventures. A straightforward style reigns, where directness is the default. Just like a child, Mercury in Aries can lead to ultra truthful comments without recognition that they might have inadvertently offended someone or hurt their feelings. The saying "open mouth insert foot" comes to mind when thinking of a person who has Mercury in Aries. There is no malice in what a Mercury in Aries person says. They just call them like they see them.

Confident speakers, Mercury in Aries enjoy public speaking and leading discussions. They definitely know how to use words to persuade others to bend to their wants. They communicate their passion and convictions like no other through their words and body language. Mercury in Aries people cannot hide their feelings. Their faces will give whatever they are feeling away so others around them buy what they are selling as their intention is obvious. The knock-on effect is the Mercury in Aries people are perceived as being very trustworthy. These qualities support strong leadership. And if someone does not acquiesce to their persuasiveness, they can act like a child who never stops asking for something they want. They might not express it in the same way as a child, but their perseverance and stubbornness in their communications will not go unnoticed. And like a child, their tone is more convivial, not demanding or mean spirited so it is easy to play along.

Brevity is not a natural communication style for Mercury in Aries. They enjoy expressing all their thoughts verbally or in writing. They feel the more words the better supporting their desire to communicate why what they are saying is correct.

For the most part, they communicate in a light, fun way, drawing people listening in to the conversation. Strong, combative communication enters into the picture when they feel they are literally in a battle for something. In this scenario, they might not even be passionate about the topic, but Mercury in Aries will not miss the opportunity to fight if provoked.

Mercury in Aries sometimes struggles with dialogue so conversations can sometimes feel one sided. Remember those born under the sign of Aries always believe their ideas, feelings, and solutions are right. Following that premise, their impulsive nature inhibits their ability to reign in their thoughts, sharing those thoughts when the time is best in a conversation instead of at the moment, they had them. Excitement for their own ideas to be heard drives their interruptions not rudeness, but the receiver of the communication might feel unheard and disconnected to what is being said. This is an Achilles Heel for the Mercury in Aries. When a Mercury in Aries person feels this disconnection in the conversation, their natural tendency is to talk more, to convince more, to share more instead of recognizing it as a moment to stop and let the other person share as well. They do not naturally recognize by pausing their stream of words, they gain more influence with the other person by bringing them back into the conversation.

Mercury in Aries tremendously enjoy having the last word in a conversation. Sorry for the repetition, but they do think they are right, leading to the need for having the last say regardless of the situation. Whether it is saying a convivial goodbye to a friend on the phone, a heated argument or a business presentation, the impulse to close seeps in. Depending on how this aspect manifests, having the last word can be useful, but it can also lead to discord.

The thought process of a Mercury in Aries person focuses on beginnings: new ideas, something no one has ever seen before, and innovation. It is very creative. They start things often, touch the surface of it, learn what they can at that surface level, and then tend to move on. Keeping a Mercury in Aries engaged means giving them the ability to build new on top of what exists even if what exists is not yet complete. Mercury in Aries people possess quick minds and can take in mounds of information, assess it quickly, and communicate it in a clear way, which is why they are gifted at leading a meeting, discussion, or presentation. They are quick on their feet where no question, whether anticipated or not, will throw them off balance.

Inspired Transformation

To improve their communication skill overall, Mercury in Aries must commit to replacing the "me" in their thoughts with "them." The more they think of others first, the more they will be heard. Here are five transformation tips to help the Mercury in Aries harness their communication skills.

1. Be patient. Work to allow others to finish their thoughts before jumping in. Instead of talking, take a deep breath or find another way to bide your time before having your say. In that moment, you might hear something that will inform your thinking to your benefit.

2. Being right is not always the point when it comes to delivering a message. Let go of what is right (this will be the hard part!) and look for what is best to achieve what you want to through this communication. Also remember the phrase "I told you so" is rarely appreciated. If you were right, celebrate internally!

3. Use your passionate communication style to inspire others, not just persuade. This is the attribute of a true leader and a way to expand the reach of your vision as more people feel a part of it.

4. Focus your communication. Sometimes more is not more, less is. Enough said!
5. Think before you speak or write. Even a heartbeat's pause helps to cure the foot-in-mouth disease.

Taurus

Imagine a beautiful field with lush, green grass sprinkled with dew, the sun shining brightly, and a warm breeze wafting across the field, maintaining the perfect temperature to keep any living creature perfectly comfortable. Within this field sits a very large fenced-in area where a bull chomps on the grass and basks in the sun. The bull can see that over the fence exists more lush fields and maybe even some shady trees, but he contentedly continues to enjoy the place he is in, never wanting to chase what is beyond his fence. The bull firmly believes this space is perfect despite the fact he is stuck unable to roam free because the fence has no gate. He does nothing to break the fence down because he has what he needs, and that is enough. This is the energy of the Taurus: comfortable, desiring little change, and being content with just enough.

The best part of the scenario I have described is that Taurians can find beauty in any situation, and they will find their feet no matter where they are. They are an Earth Sign with an internal energy of Fire, which translates into a very stable personality with moments of intensity and a desire more aligned with other Fire Signs. Willingness to hard work and persistence in the face of challenges shape the personality of a Taurian. They are dependable and will see any process through to the end. It is not unusual to see a Taurian in the same job for decades, and they are often seen as the "go to" person in any organization.

Nature is a Taurian's favorite drug. If they can feel the ground or hug a tree, they will be soothed and relaxed. The beauty of nature is likely to be surrounding them inside and outside as they seek to bring nature into their home decor. They have green thumbs, so their homes likely feel like a lush garden.

While there is nothing wrong with the picture I painted of a bull comfortable in his small field, it can act as a virtual prison for the Taurian. The bull loves to be safe and stable in its beautiful pen; however, life equals motion, and change is inevitable so the desire to keep things as they are translates into stubbornness and resistance or even aversion to change. This results in Taurians getting stuck in work, relationships, and other challenging life patterns. Because they will make the best of even the worst situations, seeing their sunny field as being enough, they will endure more than most could or should. They might also miss out on more because they tend to be satisfied, especially if more means they would have to change something they are doing. A Taurian's karmic debt is literally to be continually looking for ways to get out of their comfort zone. Taurians tend to be risk averse, taking only very calculated risks where the payoff stands a better-than-average chance of occurring. This makes them great yet conservative businesspeople and keeps them middle of the road in every other area. With this attribute, they might be leaving a lot on the table never really achieving the heights they could.

A Taurian's even-keeled temperament has its limits, so watch out if you push a Taurian beyond that point. The internal fire element will have the bull seeing red, attacking without thinking about the fallout. A "bull in a china shop" scenario comes to mind. Indiscriminate destruction metaphorically results, and more than the direct object of the Taurian's ire can be caught in the reaction. Fortunately, once a Taurian expresses their anger and it abates, they return to the pre-outburst status.

Taurians' financial acumen rates highly. Money usually flows to them, and they manage it well. Taurus ranks as one of the top signs for prosperity with the internal fire aspect keeping their desire for more high. When it comes to money, Taurians are more motivated to expand their horizons, which they could capitalize in other areas if they embraced internal transformation more.

Taurus also represents a strong connection to health and healing. Earth Signs in general and Taurians more specifically, understand nature as an unending source of healing. They are amazing healers in both traditional and nontraditional medicine.

Mercury in Taurus

Mercury in Taurus generally exhibits a calm, stable, noninflammatory communication. A steadiness exhibits the thought behind the words a Taurus chooses. A Taurus' words exude an air of expertise in anything they are talking about because they will do their homework. They do not want to be called out on something they have said incorrectly, so one can count on the fact they have double-checked their work. Confidence oozes from their communication because speaking frivolously belies their comfort level. One can depend on the fact that a Mercury in Taurus person has taken the time to support their assertions. Research actually holds a prominent place in the heart of a Mercury in Taurus. Research satisfies their fiery curiosity and helps them feel grounded in their knowledge.

Mercury in Taurus people paint beautiful pictures with their words especially in their written communications, and writing can be a passion for them. They also enjoy reading books, contracts, and other legal documents, anything they can dig into. They can sit and read for hours! What a comfortable joy for a person sporting Mercury in Taurus, so you might find people with this aspect to be research scientists, law clerks or lawyers (not litigators), or connected to real estate.

Personal communication from a Mercury in Taurus person will present as loving and flowery. They enjoy reflecting the beauty they see in the world to others, especially those they are fond of or love.

Mercury in Taurus can represent a stubbornness in communication that can act as a deterrent for collaboration. The stubbornness here does not mimic the attitude of a Mercury in Aries, who thinks they are right about everything. It stems from a place of picking a lane and not wanting to change it, regardless of the outcome. Even if there is evidence to indicate otherwise, a Mercury in Taurus person can reactively remain unmovable. The thought of changing position is extremely untenable, and therefore it can be a major roadblock to a process. They will express this via sustained, consistent communication, which also can be off-putting to people around them. When collaborating with a Mercury in Taurus person, building consensus with them at the beginning of the process before they choose a path can help ease this challenge.

Their aversion to risk will come through their communication. Their words often do not reflect their true emotions or real thoughts about something because they do not want to put themselves out there in any way that might be out of their comfort zone. Declaring love unexpectedly or showing the depth of their anger rarely occurs. While there might be times this is a good thing, for them it leads to miscues and misunderstandings.

Expect Mercury in Taurus to take their time delivering any form of communication. If you want it fast, do not ask this person for it. Deliberate and well thought through takes time.

And if you are looking for an out-of-the-box thinker, a Mercury in Taurus person will not fit the bill. They will take what is known and expand on it, but innovation is not in their thought process. This tried-and-true way of thinking and communicating represents an area of growth for the Mercury in Taurus

Inspired Transformation

To improve their communication skill overall, taking risks and expressing their underlying passions will allow Mercury in Taurus to evolve. Pushing themselves to expand their horizons and be open to change in themselves and others will help them to see better results sooner. Here are five transformation tips to help the Mercury in Taurus harness their communication skills.

1. Stop being stubborn. Your points will be heard and a little movement one way or the other will only make the process more collaborative and the outcomes more fruitful.
2. Allow yourself to take a risk every now and then as you share information. Drop a metaphorical bomb in the conversation or in a communique and see what happens just for the fun of it.

3. Embrace change and do not think that the way you see it is the final best answer. Allow yourself the luxury of changing your mind in how you say things and the path on which you are on.
4. Let your passion show through your words, even if the topic might be dry and straightforward. Your passion will drive consensus and excitement in your collaborations.
5. Give yourself tighter deadlines to practice letting go of the need to over deliberate and allowing for new ideas to start to flow.

Gemini

Ever see a bee moving from flower to flower, never landing on one for very long, seemingly in a never-ending quest for pollen? If you have ever seen a human doing that, then Gemini probably figures prominently in their chart. Geminis generally convey a very happy-go-lucky energy, attracting many people into their orbit. This is a good thing because Geminis get bored easily, so maintaining a large circle of friends keeps them happy and engaged. Quick-witted and adept with words, Geminis keep people coming back for more, especially as they don't seem to be egotistical about it. They love making people happy and keeping them laughing.

Geminis showcase their intellect whenever they can-- because they can. They are extremely smart and voracious learners. They enjoy knowing a little bit about a lot of things, which is fortunate for them because they have a lot of brain capacity to maintain a vast amount of information. Not only can they hold the data they collect, but they process information at warp speed. Speed in everything exudes from a Gemini in everything they do. Patience is literally their Achilles Heel. When an idea comes to them, they jump on it, without thought or fear of what jumping in might mean. They have confidence they will be able to turn on a dime in any situation so jumping in quickly produces no fear. And quite frankly, they do have the ability to react quickly to a situation making changes on the fly.

Gemini is an Air Sign, and their internal energy is air as well, so nothing keeps a Gemini down. Constant motion encompasses their daily routine running from one activity to another, until they eventually drop from exhaustion. Logic rules the sign Gemini, and their skill for connecting dots and showing the most logical route to a solution exceeds all other signs of the Zodiac. This logic translates into superlative communications as we will soon see. Geminis live in the strategic realm, viewing every situation from 30,000 feet involving themselves in the big picture, rarely stepping foot on the ground. They need support to manifest in business and in life in general. Remember, they also get bored very easily as well, and they fly in the big picture!

The sign of Mercury is known as the sign of the twins, which reflects the attribute Geminis embody of changing their minds and their moods quickly and frequently. One minute, a Gemini will be content and just as quickly they can explode in anger. And then the next minute they can be perfectly happy again. One minute, they desire one thing, the next minute they want the opposite. One minute, they say they want to move in one direction, the next minute they do a U-turn. This minute-to-minute swing presents confusion to those close to a Gemini and can cause unnecessary conflict or hurt. The swings are rarely a result of something personal; the Gemini is just being Gemini.

Financially, Geminis can struggle to save the money they earn because their desire for lots of things and experiences saps their resources. Their confidence that they will have more money and their high intelligence ensures that money will flow. Geminis would do well to have financial advisors around them who keep them from letting their fortune fall through their hands.

Relationships, particularly romantic ones, present a challenge for Geminis. They enjoy the giving and receiving that any relationship produces, but they shrink when faced with long-term commitment. Geminis are known for having many short-term relationships and business partnerships and multiple marriages. I will say it again: They get bored very quickly. One way to keep a Gemini committed is to keep the relationship moving all the time. Keeping up with and engaging the Gemini aids them in staying in the relationship longer. But trying to corral them in any way virtually guarantees they will abandon the situation. Give them their space, keep things interesting, give them lots to do, and you stand a chance!

Mercury in Gemini

Mercury, the Roman god of translators, served as the messenger for the gods. Speed was essential in his capacity as messenger, and it is not surprising that Mercury in Gemini people are quick in mind and quick in tongue. Their seemingly off-the-cuff comments can bring a room to gut-wrenching laughter, gut-wrenching fear, gut-wrenching excitement, or gut-wrenching worry. Their words are that powerful--even without them realizing they are. Logic rules their communication style, making it direct and focused and sometimes a little sharp in tone. They don't mean to be sharp, but they can lose patience if they have to explain something more than once because they feel everyone should process information in the same efficient way they do.

Mercury in Gemini claims the top spot for messaging accuracy, perfected tone (when they are not frustrated), and engaging delivery. They quite literally have the whole communication package when it comes to sharing information. They are like the press secretary of the universe. What they offer will make perfect sense. They lay information out clearly, logically and seamlessly connecting the dots between disparate points, bringing them all together in a neat package digestible to all.

Their effortless cleverness adds a distinctive flare of humor to their delivery that can keep even the most difficult topics light. In addition, because they love to learn even more than a non-Mercury in Gemini (note this is a purposeful duplication), their communication pulls from multidisciplinary references, which boosts the depth and interest in the topic at hand, adding elements of surprise for the recipients. Advanced communication is literally their superpower--both written and verbal.

A Mercury in Gemini person can out-logic even the most logical person because of their expansive base of knowledge and ability to create effective, supportable arguments on the fly. Do not confront a Mercury in Gemini without extensive preparation because the odds are not on the side of beating them in the debate game. They willingly and sometimes very eagerly share their expansive knowledge and can be an excellent source of information directly or by their ability to guide one to source material. Research is fun for them, and learning is a default setting in the operating system.

However, even the most desired superpowers contain chinks in the armor, and the Mercury in Gemini communication excellence is no exception. For all their intellect and wisdom, they lack the ability to access their heart in the process. Devoid of emotion, their communications can feel as if a sentient mechanical lifeform produced them, sapping them of deeper purpose and meaning to the recipient. The information is spot-on but the underlying vibe that helps recipients internalize what is being said and processing it themselves to reach the more significant meaning is missing. Mercury in Gemini scrapes the surface of emotions through their humor and lighthearted delivery, but that does not always cut it for people who long to feel their passions, concerns, joy, anger, or sadness beneath the perfect words. Because Geminis in general struggle to access their heart and share their emotions, Mercury in Gemini struggles mightily with it. Particularly, they often do not see the logic in bringing their emotions to their communication. They are blind to the power emotions add to facts, the context emotions set up for the recipient, and the way in which emotion and vulnerability open up listeners to embrace all communication, but especially that which might be more difficult to take in. They just do not get it!

This point is the single most important area for growth of the Mercury in Gemini. When they start to access it, they elevate their game from metaphorical press secretary to metaphorical leader--with the ability to pull most people who hear them to their side. For them, emotions have the most significant impact on their already amazing gift. Accessing emotions has the knock-on effect of lessening the one emotion they do bring out often: frustration with others. More emotion leads to more compassion and empathy for others, which allows for patience and understanding to bubble up from the Mercury in Gemini, softening potentially negative exchanges with others around them.

Inspired Transformation

Funny enough, there is not much to say when it comes to helping a Mercury in Gemini elevate their communication skills. The word is emotions. If you tap into your emotions and express them through your words, you will succeed every time.

1. Dig deep. Your heart is in there, and it is aching to be exposed. Do not be afraid. Emotions will enhance your ability to get your point across.
2. Open your heart. Sprinkle your passions in with your communications. People like to see what moves you.
3. Emote. Put a metaphorical ache in your words. People will jump on board to support your cause.
4. Feel the room. When you open your heart, you will be able to access the mood of the room and align your communications, better shaping them for the audience at hand.
5. Do I need to say it again?

Cancer

The crab represents the sign of Cancer in the Zodiac and highlights the essences of the Cancerian person. A crab has a very hard shell on the outside, but on the inside they are very, very soft. Another distinctive crab quality is how they move. Crabs move sideways. They do not move straight forward. In a person born under the sign of Cancer, these qualities play out in how they show up in the world and how they move through it.

The hard outer shell of a crab protects their fragile, vulnerable soft inside from predators. In the same way, the seemingly strong front Cancerians put out to the world hides a much more emotional inner core to protect themselves from getting hurt. Cancer is a Water Sign, and Cancerians are very, very emotional, but they do not like to show their emotions because that might make them vulnerable to the potential pain that vulnerability might cause them. So, they try to hide their emotions at every step. They live in their heart, feeling everything, trying not to cry, trying not to show they are weak. What they fail to recognize is their connection to their heart and their emotions is their superpower.

Cancer is by ruled the Moon. The Moon, as was shared, represents our emotional side and is therefore a Cancerian experiences repetitive ebbing and flowing of their emotions. One minute, happiness abounds, and the next minute, depression reigns in their hearts. Tears commonly show up on a Cancerian's facial canvas. Causing a Cancerian to want to cry is simple, just utter a soft word, show affection, or criticize them. But like the crab, they use their outer shell, their external self, as protection and will fight the tears from flowing, but this battle will not last long, and sooner rather than later the tears will seep out.

Cancerians are very, very connected to their homes. Home provides them a sense of security and safety, just like the crab's outer shell. They take pride in their surroundings, the home they built, the room they sleep in, their office. Wherever that is, big or small it will be beautiful and comfortable like a security blanket.

Cancerians pride themselves on being risk averse, which links to their desire to feel safe and secure. They will not take big risks, and for sure their risks will be calculated. They understand the value of taking risks, and they might easily follow others into taking risk if a leader or situation exists that they believe in and if they see others taking the first step into that direction. They will follow, but very rarely will be out in front. Going back to the attribute of the crab who must move sideways, taking risk and leading equates to direct thought and action and that is very difficult for a Cancerian to do. To be clear, they can make great leaders because of the strong connection and intuition about circumstances and people's emotions but choose not to lead because of the discomfort they think they will feel being in that position. They always will revert to what is going to be the safest place for them where they are the most secure. Cancerians often find themselves working in middle management. Cancerians drive for a promotion at work will be shaped by their perception of whether their work security in that role is guaranteed. If a new role feels like it could be a new "home" for them at work, they feel safe, little risk exists then they will go for it.

Big homebodies Cancerians prefer to be at home almost more than anyplace else. Their connection to their family and friends is extremely important to them. They pour everything they are into their relationships. And the interesting thing is, even if you are not family by blood or marriage, if they consider you like family, they act in an equivalent manner as they would for their own child. There literally is no difference.

Being in the aura of a Cancerian can be very enriching. The flip side of being a recipient of what Cancerians offer is what they offer might be very overwhelming. They tend to give more than is wanted or even when it is not appropriate. They can be a little overbearing, like a mother who pushes food on her child even when they are not hungry. The kid might feel full and run away from the situation and the mom, avoiding an uncomfortable scenario. Cancerians sometimes lack balance in their giving, so they must be careful about how they share their love.

Relationships are key to Cancerians feeling safe and secure so again, lack of balance shines through. Clinging to people and using them to provide a sense of self and security commonly arises in Cancerian relationships. Likewise, making a straightforward decision activates discomfort, so they often stay longer in a relationship or circumstance longer than they should.

Cancerians can be very good businesspeople. Money flows around them, and they also are financially very sound. Cancerians make amazing designers, therapists, social workers, and teachers. Any career where they can connect with people or create beauty in physical locations works for them. They save their money and plan for the future, investing to ensure they will have what they need. They do not want to feel like they are out on a limb on anything. Their financial acumen comes from a survival perspective, not from a growth perspective or having a big desire to be a multimillionaire. It all comes from their instinct to be safe and secure.

Being a Water Sign with their internal energy imbues Cancerians with very deep instinctive qualities not found in the other elements. Cancerians are incredibly intuitive and connected to the vibrations of physical locations. A Cancerian can walk into a place and feel its energy, knowing if it is positive or negative and how the space might impact what goes on in it. It's like the walls somehow speak to them about all that has gone on. They don't always allow themselves to connect with that deep level of intuition and connection to the metaphysical because it can be a little overwhelming and scary. They are often unsure what to make of their skill. But when they do allow themselves to open up and recognize the power of their connection to the metaphysical and their ability to really feel people in situations, they thrive. But tapping into that intuition requires effort because first they have to feel safe and comfortable in that setting. Consequently, many Cancerians miss out on the benefit of their psychic abilities.

Mercury in Cancer

Cancerians live in their heart and direct, logical thinking eludes them. Their thought process is a little bit all over the place and driven by emotion--not their head. Therefore, Mercury in Cancer leads from emotion, how they are feeling about something not what they think about it. A conversation with a Mercury in Cancer forces you to check in on your feelings as well no matter how much you might push them to engage in a direct line of thinking. A debate with a Mercury in Cancer might end in your victory, but it might not be sweet because although you might have out-thought them, you possibly took an unwanted emotional journey to get there.

Everything about a Mercury in Cancer's communications is going to be filled with their emotions, but stifled emotion. Remember, they are trying to protect themselves and stay safe. If they perceive their emotion will expose any weakness, even a sensed weakness, they will retreat into minimal communication or even deceptive communication. So, their communications result in a bit of indirectness. They dance around their thoughts, using words to hide what they think you will not take well. For example, if they must correct your actions, they shy away from saying something like, "You have done this wrong." They sprinkle platitudes into their communication to soften the blow or distract from the real message.

Another defense mechanism they avail themselves of is to start off very hard and then backtrack. They want to be perceived as strong and straight-forward like the crab with their shell, projecting confidence and conviction in what they are communicating instead of revealing their true position. This style of communication might be off-putting and result in an unanticipated or unwanted reaction, cracking their external defenses and causing them to cave to others' positions rather than standing their ground knowing their point of view is valid. This quality does not prove successful in heated negotiations.

It can also result in them receiving much less than they desire or deserve.

A Mercury in Cancer finds it difficult to sustain the hard-shell mask, so they are easy to break, getting to their soft middle. They avoid confrontations and hard conversations at all costs. They want to make things feel safe and secure for everybody. Their communications start with asking about the other person or people, ensuring they are comfortable and happy. They need to make a connection, which can be very powerful in a lot of ways because it provides them the opportunity to align with where the other person is at. Even if the communication is written, the receiver senses the care on display, dispelling any sense of negativity or hard feelings. A Mercury in Cancer person can wipe that stuff away with their words.

Their words express the depth of their emotions and knowledge. Mercury in Cancer people make amazing authors because they love to use words to paint pictures of their imagination. They appreciate the intensity of a word. For example, they will know twenty words to describe happiness, and they will use them. Being able to express their deep emotions using many words allows them a sense of security in how they are presenting themselves.

With so much depth in what and how they communicate, brevity and speed never appear. It might take them a while to get there, but they will get there. You are not going to have a quick conversation with a Mercury in Cancer. You are going to have to go with them on the journey. Deep conversations are a standard operating procedure for them. They do not want to say a quick hello. Conversations offer an opportunity to engage in an emotional connection, and that takes time.

Because a Mercury in Cancer struggles with forthrightness, hidden meanings get sprinkled in their communications, masking what they are really trying to say. It can be a guessing game trying to figure out what is real fact and what are emotions clouding reality. Their lack of straightforwardness can be extremely frustrating and a challenge for others.

In addition, Mercury in Cancer people hide behind words and blur the truth a little bit. Going back to the idea of protecting themselves, they might put forward ideas or thoughts that lead in another direction, ensuring their truth is not on display. If you know a Mercury in Cancer person, make sure their work is double-checked or assume there might be more to the story than is being shared. Misdirection is always a possibility. Remind yourself when Mercury in Cancer is speaking or writing that in the back of their mind they are thinking, *How can I keep myself safe in this situation? How can I protect myself?* Again, checking facts with them is super important.

Inspired Transformation

Inspiration transformation for Mercury in Cancer revolves around letting their guard down and trusting in the strength of their emotions and intuition. When they balance the hard shell with the soft insides, their communication with others will more often result in fruitful, prosperous outcomes, leaving everyone in a balanced state.

1. Drop the protection shields. Hiding does not protect you for long. Put your emotions out there with confidence because even if the result of putting yourself out there directly is undesirable, it will serve you more in the long run.
2. Focus on communicating your thoughts more directly. Practice writing and communicating in as few words as possible. This will help you learn how to soften the emotions behind what you are trying to say.
3. The whole truth will set you free, so stop bending it to what you feel someone will want to hear or you think they need to hear to bend them to your will. Present the facts as they are because at the end of the day, reshaping the truth will not really bring you what you want.
4. Remember, confidence in your communication is not the same thing as being forceful or strong in proving your point. Confidence is conveyed by your passion and

emotional connection to what you are communicating. Start softer and give others the chance to be brought into your amazing ideas.

5. Use your emotions to bring people along with you and connect with where they are at. Your emotions are your superpower, and your intuition is strong. Trust yourself to converse and communicate how you feel without thinking you are weak.

Leo

Imagine a beautiful African plain with trees dotting the horizon under an amazingly blue sky with sunlight shining on everything. Sitting on a high cliff overlooking the plain sits a statuesque lion or lioness, viewing their expansive realm with contentment washing over them. With that picturesque scene in mind, you can imagine a little bit about the essence of a Leo--majestic, proud, and very connected to the land in which they feel they reign. Leo is a Fire Sign ruled by the Sun with the internal energy of fire as well. Leo is a very powerful sign, and those born under the sign feel very much like the Sun in they bring life, sustenance, joy, and prosperity.

Leos take leadership to the next level. They can engage people, persuade people, build consensus, dictate to people, and applaud themselves--while still being likeable and amiable, akin to being a part of the crowd while still ruling over them.

They're very benevolent, generous people who truly want the best for everyone. They want people to feel the rays of the sunlight they feel they embody, and they are always attracting people into their realm. People enjoy feeling their energy and being around it. You know a Leo has arrived the minute they walk into a room because their presence is naturally commanding. Being the center of attention brings comfort to a Leo. They are very proud of who they are, and they love to talk about themselves, sharing their adventures and accomplishments.

Believe it or not, even with all the fire energy they have, Leos can be very, very lazy, not in that they lack motion, but in their approach and attitude. They possess an air of entitlement where others should do for them rather than do it themselves. They enjoy being served, and they often will sit back and let themselves be taken care of in a lot of ways.

A Leo's laziness extends to their internal growth as well. They operate through a belief system telling them they have already arrived, and they question why they would need to do anything more. Leos are very effective at convincing the people around them to pick up their slack because those people seek the sun the Leo has to offer. However, if a Leo continues to rely on others in this way, they might be confronted with the support group abandoning them as the Leo egocentricity starts to wear on even the most stalwart fan.

Leos are strategic. Their view of the world is from on high and drives them to map out how they can conquer a situation. Leos do not often get into the nitty-gritty, in that tactical space where the doers are getting things done. They prefer to visualize a plan and send others to do the work. Creativity abounds in the Leo mind. They think up incredible ideas and are very innovative, often seeing things before others have the chance to catch it because their vision is so broad. They want to give back to the world and will provide for people and put themselves out there for others if they can particularly because it brings with it something they require more than material things--acknowledgement and accolades.

A challenging aspect of the Leo personality finds itself in the quid pro quo mentality attached to their generosity and benevolence. When they do something for others, they expect they will receive something in return for their altruism. And that something can be as simple as acknowledgement their actions are valuable. They want to be acknowledged, they want to be thanked, and they want you to know you are in their debt in case they require something in the future. Did I mention that Leos make natural politicians?

When acknowledgement falls by the wayside, a Leo's ire goes up, and their generosity and mercy take a nosedive. A Leo can fixate for days on how they were mistreated by the recipient who failed to pay the proper accolade, taking them away from productive thoughts and work. Because acknowledgement and accolades are so important to a Leo, decisions might be made by assessing where they will receive more of both instead of looking at what might be the best opportunity for them in general.

For example, let's say a Leo is looking to buy an office building as an investment. They have two options: One is a tall building that everyone knows but is 50 percent occupied, and the other is a smaller unknown building that is 95 percent occupied. The smaller building clearly offers a higher potential for a larger return, but the Leo would look at the well-known building and say, "I want that one, and I will show everyone how I can make it work financially." The well-known building provides the Leo with the opportunity to literally point to it with pride, making it easier for others to validate and provide accolades more than the unknown building. A Leo will sacrifice conservative strategy for the risk of a bigger payout that feeds their ego. Chasing that accolade and validation might lead to unfortunate results that are not what the Leo thought that they were going to be.

Another way this need for acknowledgement gets in the way is in relationships with people, both personally and professionally. The Leo can get either very angry or dismissive if someone does not return a gesture. The Leo expects this, and when it does not happen or happens in a way less than the Leo expected, they might quickly, effectively cut them out.

Also because Leos are like the Sun, they radiate in amazing ways, and not everyone is capable of, or desires to do that. So, when they set expectations about what others should be doing and a person does not live up to it because they do not know how, the Leo can be very, very disappointed, disconnect themselves, and ultimately find themselves in a lonely situation.

Like a king or queen who has trusted advisors who help guide them, Leos benefit greatly when they allow a few people they trust to support them. Even though they feel they can do anything, there are many skills a Leo does not have. A Leo can really thrive by surrounding themselves with people who complement their skills and being willing to seek and follow their advice. It is not easy for a Leo to succumb to other's input, but it is vitally necessary to their ability to grow to greater heights. By trusting others, the Leo can be more balanced, less reactive, and feel less the need for outside acknowledgement.

As long as they're willing to allow others around them to shine their light, not blotting it out by their own light, they excel.

Leos are very decisive. They identify what they want, and they quickly figure out how to obtain it. However, they lack an internal system for processing their emotions. They are driven by what they want, what they need, and how they are going to be acknowledged for what they accomplish. A large part of their transformational work is learning how to allow their true emotions to come through.

In relationships, the Leo loves and gives as long as they feel they are ruling the relationship while receiving an abundance of attention. They will not do well in a relationship with somebody who needs as much as attention as they do because then that ends up being a battle of the egos. They can cut off a relationship very quickly if they feel not enough attention is being paid to them. They have a lot of pride, which can be destructive to their relationships, particularly if their partner lacks the flair of flattery.

Financially, Leos usually do very well, often naturally attracting money into their life. However, they are not adept at holding onto their money for very long. Their generosity drives them to spend as does their need to be seen. They will buy things so people notice them, like an expensive or unique car. They might not need it, but they buy it because they want to be noticed driving down the street. Again, if they have a trusted advisor around them who manages their money habits, they will do a whole lot better.

Mercury in Leo

When it comes to communication, everything about how Leos communicate is big. They are very dramatic. There's no small Leo anything. They will not say anything quietly nor subtly. Drama finds a home in the way a Mercury in Leo communicates. A Mercury in Leo will also insert themselves in the context of what they are communicating because they like to talk about themselves. For example, if a Mercury in Leo is writing a cookbook they might share the directions for how to make the pizza, but they will spend ten pages talking about where they found the pizza, how they learned to make the pizza, how many attempts they had to make, how they felt about how to do it, and how to make it correctly instead of just sharing the recipe.

A lot of energy comes through a Mercury in Leo's communications, and it is not uncommon for people to struggle to take it all in because it is big and dramatic and often loud. When I say loud, I am not necessarily speaking about volume, but rather the word choice and how they express them can be metaphorically loud and full of passion on hyperdrive. Mercury in Leo sense if they withhold their passion that people won't feel the same way as they do about something. It's difficult for Mercury in Leo to tone it down, allowing everybody to hear what they are saying. They love to weave a story so one might find the dialogue with a Mercury in Leo is not that short.

Leo's confidence when they communicate rates highly. Everything shared by a Mercury in Leo will be dripping with their confidence and exhibit their logical thinking. They're not going to mince words. The words might be very flowery, and the Mercury in Leo might take a long time to say what they want to say because they are interspersing their communique with themselves, but in the end, you will know what they want and what they're telling you to do. They are very decisive, and their communication reflects that decisive nature.

A Mercury in Leo's communication style is akin to a leader pronouncing an edict. They do not ask; they tell. Their communication will boil down to how they want things to happen, and if you do not like it, you can go away.

Communication from a Mercury in Leo is going to be highly punctuated, and so you need to be prepared to feel the heat of their energy as they communicate. They use their hands a lot when they are speaking. Big sweeping motions with their hands will almost be like a running dialogue under their spoken words. Watching their body language as they speak will help to decipher their intensity or lack thereof in what they are saying. In writing, the communication is usually long. Where they insert themselves in the context exhibits their passion.

If you know a Mercury in Leo (or actually any Leo), one of the best strategies you can use to open up a productive dialogue is to start the conversation by paying them a compliment. Remember Leos generally seek acknowledgement, and when Mercury is in Leo a well-placed compliment can open the lines of communication in a way that garners more of the Leo benevolence to your advantage.

This is a great negotiating tool with a Mercury in Leo. When it feels like negotiations are going in the wrong direction, toss out a compliment, and the Mercury in Leo will not be able to avoid taking the bait and give something back in return. In addition, a Mercury in Leo person truly enjoys being asked about their opinion, so asking for that opinion is another good way to provide acknowledgement, opening the door for a fruitful conversation even if it might have to be a difficult one.

Inspired Transformation

The best way for a Mercury in Leo to enhance their communication skills overall is to add a bit of humility into it. What you have to say is important and should be heard, but injecting humility into it allows those important messages to come through to more people.

1. Tone it down. Learn how to whisper more meaning so you can say less and create an even bigger impact across a larger group of people.
2. Take yourself out of it. Try to communicate without making it all about you. Put yourself in others' shoes and contemplate how they would like to hear from you.
3. Express your passion--not your pride. Your energy is infectious, and that is what people want to hear about.
4. Be clear about your expectations of what you want in return. You might be direct about where you want to go but not about what you want from people to get you there. If you need a specific response, ask for it and then be okay if you do not get it in the way you want.
5. Don't pronounce, ask. Show your openness to others' opinions. Think about how you are asking for what you need so you can leave room for dialogue.

Virgo

The lens through which Virgos see the world looks like a pure, white blank canvas ready to be enlivened by the imagination of an artist. The canvas is perfect when blank, and their desire is to carry that perfection through to final art. For a Virgo, precision, refinement, discernment, fine details, and perfection offer comfort and a place for them to excel. Virgos notice everything, even those things most of us will miss. For example, they can spot a minute speck of dirt on a large, white tablecloth where others would just see the tablecloth as spotless. The term Virgo originates from the word virgin, so it is not surprising that Virgos appreciate and connect to pureness and perfection.

Virgos can hone in on the smallest flaws and figure out how to fix them to bring them back to a purer state. For a Virgo, it is all about returning the world to the state of perfection, which they already see. They actually can see the world in its perfected state, and they see people in their perfected state. They desire for everyone and everything to get to that point so happiness can reign. Their quest is a noble one, and it's one they take seriously whether they are aware of it or not.

As a result of this weighty mission, Virgos embrace and deliver judgement as their primary tool to push us all to the point of perfection. They hunt for flaws and quickly point them out to the perpetrator, whomever it might be, including themselves. More often than not, they are absolutely correct about what the flaw is and how it can be remedied. However, true perfection is nearly impossible to achieve, so Virgos can spend a lifetime chasing something unattainable, leading to a sense of overall ultimate disappointment.

Virgo is an Earth Sign combined with the internal element of air. They are grounded and stable, and emotional swings and extremes rarely appear. Although they might be very passionate about something, they project an air of calmness so it might be difficult to truly understand what excites them. In fact, Virgos seek to maintain that sense of calmness in everything. Loudness, boisterousness, over-the-top behavior, chaos, and crowds all disturb their sensibility. They prefer peacefulness, cleanliness, simplicity, and serenity. Their underlying air element reflects in Virgo's high intellect and ability to communicate, which belies their external persona as they tend to be more introverted.

Virgos are clean-a-holics. Everything around them must be put in their proper place whatever place that is. They want to see things in a beautiful state. Mess and disarray produce extreme discomfort. Virgos do have a little obsessive compulsive disorder when it comes to their spaces and personal hygiene. You will know when you walk into a Virgo home because it will be tidy, neat, and beautiful whatever the décor. They will probably ask you to leave your shoes at the door and refrain from touching certain items in their house!

Even though Virgos routinely point out others' flaws to push them to their perfection, Virgos are determined to achieve perfection in their own lives as well. They expect much of themselves and what they deliver in the world, and if they fall short in their mind, they will beat themselves up relentlessly. That is unhealthy, plus chasing perfection acts as a roadblock to achieving anything, so Virgos often stall in their work to achieve their goals. For example, they might have the drive to write a book, but it will take years to finish it because they edit, re-edit, and re-edit it again. They can be the obstacle on a team to deliver a project on time because their part is not yet perfect. It can even cause them to not seek to do something new because they fear they will not ever be able to achieve perfection in that arena. New opportunities can come and go as the Virgo sidelines themselves for fear they will fall short of perfection. Quitting before completion is another common action a Virgo takes when they feel they might fall short of where they want to be.

Virgos struggle to recognize a process must exist to reach perfection, and that process is littered with imperfection, which is ultimately perfect and as it should be. Imperfection promotes perfection because it shows us what we need to do to get to perfection. Unfortunately, Virgos often miss that important part of their journey.

The drive for perfection is a very difficult edge to round out for Virgos when it comes to themselves--and also in their relationships. Expectations run high, and Virgos struggle to keep their thoughts about someone's shortfalls to themselves. People in their universe might hear their critiques as they are never going to be good enough—that they are never going to be a good enough friend, child, or parent, whatever that is. Rebellion against perfection by the recipient can lead to a cycle of critique, rebellion, and critique because the distance from perfection increases.

Even with the high bar, Virgos thrive in close relationships, remaining loyal and loving, precisely because they see the beauty of every soul around them. Once a person passes the test, Virgos commit, and they stay committed. They are wonderful sources of advice and support, and they will always be there for those that need them. They value their solitude and definitely require their own space to retreat to, but they do not mind joining in on parties and events--so long as they are civilized.

Financially, Virgos earn steadily and save well. They desire comfort, so frivolity does not come into the picture. Entrepreneurs would do well to ensure there is a Virgo amongst their team because they will provide guardrails for financial stability without requiring stinginess in spending. They understand to make business work, money needs to be spent, but with care. Virgos thrive in any career that requires precision and attention to detail. Account, architect, dental hygienist, dentist, designer, and book editor are common careers for a Virgo.

Mercury in Virgo

Mercury in Virgo equals eloquent communications. They choose their words carefully and meticulously. Each word, whether spoken or written, conveys a precise meaning, reflecting a very specific way for them to express their ideas because they believe what they say can be impactful. When they speak, they mean it, and there is no doubt that what they are saying is underpinned by knowledge they have already sought for this specific purpose.

They desire to be clearly understood as well, which leads to focused, concise communication. Their intellect and love of aesthetics shows through in their communication style. They communicate logically, driving their recipient to the outcome by using beautiful words in an aesthetically appealing manner, especially when they communicate with people they care about. Their care will shine through poetically. They can paint pictures with their words, and they are excellent at helping others visualize their points. However, the need for speed works against a Mercury in Virgo because of the particular way they communicate. Because they might be editing themselves as they speak, it will be a slow conversation. In writing, re-editing over and over again until perfection is reached can result in delays in delivery.

Mercury in Virgo communications will not miss out on any detail, ensuring the recipient receives a deep understanding of whatever topic is on the table. In fact, the communications might be detail heavy, providing an overload of information whether it has been asked for or not, which can be positive and negative, depending on the situation. With this attribute, Mercury in Virgo excels at writing documents like research reports, legal briefs, or anything else where details matter.

Someone receiving communications from a Mercury in Virgo can feel as if they are being chastised about something because Virgos tend to focus on problems that need fixing before discussing anything positive. I believe this comes from a place of encouraging perfection, not from a place of criticism, but unfortunately their communication might not be received that way, causing barriers to collaborations and hurt feelings. Unaware they might have delivered a hurtful message, a Mercury in Virgo can be shocked to learn they have been the source of pain because as they see it, they are only trying to help the person or situation be the best they can be. The perceived lack of self-awareness might add to an already fraught circumstance because the recipient might not understand how the Mercury in Virgo does not see it. This is definitely an area of growth for the Mercury in Virgo.

Inspired Transformation

Mercury in Virgo's room for growth connects to a big shift in their belief system about perfection. When they embrace the idea that imperfection is a critical part of life's process that drives us closer to our perfected state, their communications will move toward expressing their innate ability to see beauty and be more compassionate as a result.

1. Embrace imperfection. Try and not edit yourself and your work more than twice, allowing people to experience your emotions.
2. Start with the positive. Save the critiques for the second part of your communication, giving the receiver the chance to stay open to what you are saying.
3. Edit the details. Unless you are working on a research document, not everything needs to be known by everyone.
4. Practice creative writing without editing your work. Let your thoughts flow. You don't have to share it with anyone, but it will help you to let go of the need to constantly edit every word.
5. Learn the value of improvisation, which happens in the moment. Take a fun improv class where you have to respond to the last thing you hear without giving it much thought. This will help you enjoy imperfect communication. If you don't want to take a class, ask a friend or family member to interview you about a topic without letting you see the questions first. You will be on the spot and have to respond in the moment. Record it and laugh at any mistakes you might make. And P.S. you aren't allowed to bring notes!

Libra

In a world where taking sides seems to be an international sport, Libra stands as the sign of the Zodiac that worries and thinks about what is good, fair, right, and just for everyone. Librans must feel and see justice in the world, certainly in any circumstance around them. When justice eludes them, they seek to find and create some sense of balance. This drive for justice applies to everything they see on every level from their close friends and families to the world at large.

The sign of Libra is represented by scales because of their constant quest for balance. The Libran thought process requires that no one should get more than another or less than another or be treated one way, and another treated differently. Everyone should be treated equally when their circumstances seem equal.

Librans rank as the most likable sign of the whole zodiac. People want to be around them. They are smart, bright, and funny, and they have great, light energy. People feel the energy of the Libra wanting to take care of them and to make sure they are okay and being treated well.

Libra is an Air Sign, which points to high intellect, a way with words, and an insatiable interest in learning. Libra's internal element is water. Amazingly, this combination establishes a true balance between the head, where an Air Sign feels more comfortable, and the heart, where a water sign feels more comfortable. Libras are logical and compassionate at the same time, so well balanced! The internal water aspect of the Libran also gives them their signature trait: empathy.

Librans observe and experience the world from a 360-degree point of view. They constantly place themselves in another's shoes. Their perspective informs their idea that to keep everything in balance one must be able to imagine how another thinks and feels. You must be able to feel or think what

The Planet Mercury

they might be feeling or thinking to adjudicate whether or not justice endures. Librans will take the time and energy to really understand another person's experience. It is not uncommon to find Librans in the role of judge, law, politics, or advocacy because they are so concerned ensuring everyone experiences fairness.

Their gift of advocacy emanates from them. They will take the time to investigate a story, and once they understand it, they can literally almost live that story themselves and be able to build consensus around it. Even with the ability to build consensus, leadership does not come naturally because sometimes a leader is forced to make really tough decisions that go against one group or another. Not everybody can always win. The Libra vigorously looks for ways that allow everybody to win, and so it is sometimes hard for them to be put in a position where they'd have to say no or where they would have to let one side or the other down.

Librans are huge people pleasers--often to their own detriment. They embody a deep need to be liked and seen in the most positive light so if they feel somebody needs something, they offer it up without regard for their own needs. When the Libran's motivation is pure, that is truly generous and amazing. However, when the motivation arises from a need to be liked and not from a desire to bring true value to the other person, the action works against both the Libran and the person they are working to please. Misplaced people pleasing can cause the receiver to disconnect from the Libran because the receiver can feel the lack of authenticity in the action. They feel the quid pro quo.

For example, let's say a Libran mom with school-aged kids receives a great job offer, but she will have a long commute taking her away from her kids more often during the week. She struggles to decide if she should take the job. She worries her kids will not thrive if she is not home for them as often. She knows she can find the right solution, but in her heart, she feels they will be angry with her, resulting in losing their love. The likely Libran response would be to pass on the opportunity. In this example, the need to be loved clouds the Libran mom's

75

ability to go through a process where she discusses the opportunity, shares her excitement, lets her kids share their feelings, and builds a solution together that would have been healthier and more beneficial for all.

Libras are very creative thinkers, spending a lot of time trying to figure out the best solution for everyone. They think outside of the box, analyzing all sides. The downside to the Libran analysis and seeing all sides is they can be completely indecisive with too many possibilities, opportunities, and directions to take. Paralysis by analysis stops a Libran in their tracks. They worry their choice will be the wrong one because they see the benefits and pitfalls of all paths. Trying to determine which path has the most benefit or the least pitfalls frustrates progress in any of them. All this overanalyzing is attached to a decision they must make for their own life because emotions mix into the equation, with the internal water element bringing in more emotions than is typical for an Air Sign.

Paradoxically, when it comes to making decisions for other people, such as at work, a Libra's logic allows them to exhibit extreme decisiveness. When they see the logic of something, for example, if they are presented as a judge with a case, the arguments are made, and there are many things to back them up, then their assessment asks, is this fair? Is the defendant being treated in the best way? If there are penalties to be meted out, they balance what the penalty should be given what the person did, being fair to everybody concerned.

A Libra's indecisiveness can stunt their desire as well. They either want so many things that they can't decide which one, or they get stuck in the idea that they can't have everything.

The internal water element does help Librans when it comes to relationships. Once they have connected with a person, they are more stable and enjoy making a commitment. With their heightened access to their emotions, their connectiveness, empathy, and compassion are heightened as well. Once they find their person or their people, they will stick close to them.

Even though Libra is a heady sign and there's a lot of intellect behind it, they will allow their emotions to flow, which is a big reason people like to be around them. They are really, really fun to be around. They carry their happy-go-lucky, kind persona into their relationships. And the nice part is that when they land in a relationship, they are not trying to out-logic everybody like their fellow Air Signs often do.

Librans can be very financially stable. They earn nice livings, some less, some more, but their motivation is less about money and more about what they are doing and how it brings fairness into the world. You don't hear a Libra say, "I have to have it all at any cost." They like achievement, but they are happy with having enough, and they will be fine as long as everybody else in their world also has what they need. That is what drives them. Do we have enough for food on the table? Do we have enough money for our kids to do what they need to do? Is everybody happy?

Mercury in Libra

Mercury in Libra's style of communication is straightforward, yet emotional, light and airy, paralleled with their emotions. Mercury in Libra loves wordplay, which their intellect and humor allow. They might drop a pun into a conversation or pull obscure words out of their hat to the delight of others. Even when confrontation is necessary, a Mercury in Libra will find ways to soften their words and connect with the person because they want to be fair to them. You will rarely hear a harsh statement from a Mercury in Libra.

However, their communication turns dark, forceful, and reprimanding if they perceive an injustice has occurred and they want to fix it. That is when their fighting words make their appearance. The words will be biting, and the wordplay turns ominous. If they really feel like somebody needs to be put in their place, watch out, kindness will go out the window. When Mercury in Libra turns negative, the recipient should immediately realize they have done something that is being perceived as unfair, and they are being judged and convicted.

Mercury in Libra are fantastic writers. They are amazing at processing information, then infusing it with emotion, allowing more people to connect with what they are saying. They help people in difficult situations through words, and the importance of what they are saying is felt in the heart. They build consensus through their ability to connect with emotion, so persuasion is infused into much of their communication style.

Ensuring people see all sides of a story, Mercury in Libra go to great lengths to make sure that all sides are represented. Because their concern is for others and fairness, they will come into conversations humbly and conciliatory, asking what you need first. They want to hear from others before they add their own opinion. Even when upset with somebody, they ask if the person is alright first before launching into the conversation. In a conversation, second place is the best place for them.

They desire to let people be heard and are experts at interrogation in the best possible way. They know how to ask good questions that elicit the best answers. They make wonderful journalists because of their skills of inquiry and their pursuit to present every angle as well as the fairest version of any topic. Their light, breezy style invites people to explore their discourse. Public speaking comes easy. Opinion flows through their communication as does rhetoric as they seek to ensure all sides are presented. Their world view will be infused in their communication.

Inspired Transformation

Mercury in Libra offers the most balanced communication style, offering little room for correction! Overall, the theme for their transformation is to remember that not everyone is going to always be pleased, so shaking things up through your words can have immense benefits even if it does not feel comfortable.

1. Pick a lane. You do not always have to present or explore all sides. The recipients of your communication want to know where you stand. That helps them manage their end of the dialogue.
2. Allow your needs to come first and state them clearly.

3. Being too conciliatory for the sake of fairness diminishes authority when needed. Do not be afraid to upset someone. It might be exactly what they need.
4. Remember not everyone is as adept with words as you, so know your audience and how far you can go with wordplay.
5. Amp up showing your vulnerable side. Your emotions help your communications, and the more you use them, the more you will build consensus.

Scorpio

Scorpios combine firey passion with deep emotional sensitivity. Scorpio is a Water Sign with an internal element of fire, which creates an intense personality. Depth of feeling and emotion personifies them, allowing for a sensitivity to the world around them that guides their view of the world. They sense situations around them--whether they are a part of them or not. They can walk into a room and immediately read the energy of the people in the room and what is or has happened there, whether positive or negative. They will set their mood accordingly, either being open or on guard, making them extremely reactive to external factors. This attribute gives the Scorpio an innate sixth sense that guides them in ways other people find almost eerily prescient and foreboding.

The Scorpio manifest what they want. Their internal fire drives them to reach their objective, and their watery nature keeps the flame from burning out too fast, allowing them to see their desires come to fruition. Creativity abounds on every level, particularly as they are introspective and can draw from a very deep well of feeling. They can handle dark places better than most, so shining a light on them through creative expression comes naturally and results in allowing others to be more vulnerable to their own feelings. A constant connection to spirituality resides in a Scorpio whether they admit it or not because they are incredibly sensitive to the metaphysical world receiving messages regularly. They don't always accept the messages or admit they have this power, primarily because they do not understand how to deal with the power their intuition brings. They feel it, and it works for them in their life, but they don't always understand how to make it useful for them because they're almost afraid of their own power.

Scorpio own a leadership quality, but not in a traditional way. They would rather lead from behind, advising others to execute their plans than be out front. They can be both strategic and tactical, which is not a trait that another sign encompasses. This quality offers the Scorpio unique advantages when it comes to their career, business, and relationships if they play the game at the highest level. Along with creativity in their thinking, Scorpios can chart a unique path to success in whatever they want to do.

The intensity of the Scopio's nature has a few downsides, sometimes more than the other Zodiac signs have to bear. To illustrate this, I want to share an old story about a turtle that was standing by the side of a river, minding its own business. The turtle was approached by a scorpion who asked the turtle if he would carry the scorpion across the river. Now the turtle knew scorpions had a reputation for killing for no reason so he asked, "Why would I want to carry you across the river? Your sting can kill, and you scorpions have a reputation for killing indiscriminately. And I really don't want to risk my life taking you across the river, so my answer is no."

The scorpion replied, "Why want to kill you? If you take me and I kill you, I will drown too."

The turtle thought about it and said, "You know what, you're right. Because you would die too, I think I am safe, so I will take you."

The scorpion jumped on the turtle's back, and they started to cross the river. Halfway across the river and for no apparent reason, the scorpion stung the turtle. Before the turtle drowned, killing both the scorpion and the turtle, the turtle asked the scorpion, "Why would you do that? I don't understand."

The scorpion said, "It's my nature, and I can't go against my nature."

This story highlights a significant aspect of the Scorpio nature: self-destruction. If a Scorpio senses their back is in a corner, instead of fighting for a solution, they will take themselves out of the situation prematurely and sometime permanently. For example, a Scorpio hears there will be layoffs at their company. No one in management has indicated the Scorpio would be a part of the layoff, but the creative mind of the Scorpio calculates that it might make sense to the company for it to lay them off. Without any basis in reality, the Scorpio decides their head is on the chopping block and instead of waiting to see, they quit before the layoffs happen. Their quitting has two negative aspects. First, they might not have been on the layoff list and could have kept their job. Second, if they were a part of the layoff, they would have received compensation, which they missed out on because they quit. In the end, they will say they quit because it is just part of their nature even if they know it was a rash decision.

Their deep intuition can also lead to rash decisions. They might be sensing something is wrong, and they might be right, but they do not always know what they are sensing, so they do not know quite what to do with the visceral information. Instead of waiting to see what plays out, they might jump the gun. They can get hurt easily because their expectations may not be aligned with what others can realistically deliver.

Trust is not a Scorpio's strong suit. Trust must be hard earned by people around them, and even when trust has been earned, the Scorpio still believes the trust will possibly be violated. If trust is violated, a Scorpio will cut that person out of their life, period. No discussion, no mercy, no questions asked. Even if the infraction might be relatively small, the result will be the same. It is an all-or-nothing proposition. On top of that, Scorpios retain everything for a very long time. If you cross a Scorpio and they really cut you out, it is unlikely they will bring you back into their life, and they might also even seek ways to get revenge.

Relationships with Scorpios have some tricky roads to navigate. And while that is true, Scorpios love and love to be in love. Once a Scorpio allows you into their inner circle, they are fiercely loyal, supportive, and loving. They shower people they love with gifts and will be there through thick and thin. Unfortunately, sometimes Scorpios can take their love and support too far, which can be overbearing for the person on the receiving end of it. Trust is always going to play in the Scorpio's mind, so they might have a tendency to be jealous. When in a romantic relationship with a Scorpio, deliberate communication often works to ease their jealous streak.

Financially, Scorpios handle money masterfully. They attract it, hang onto it, and make it grow. Scorpios flourish when investing, connected to their sixth sense. Generosity plays a role in the Scorpio world both in money and time. They enjoy giving because seeing people thrive brings them joy. Finance, counseling and consultancy, national security, and government intelligence are all positive careers for a Scorpio as well as the creative arts.

Mercury in Scorpio

The Mercury in Scorpio communication style is underpinned by the suspicious Scorpio nature. Evasion, communicating in circles, and keeping things close to their chest are common communication practices of the Mercury in Scorpio. One might ask a simple question like, "What are you doing today?" A typical Mercury in Scorpio answer runs along the lines of, "not sure," "going out," "taking me time." Telling anything more in detail works against their nature in a big way. The term "on a need-to-know" basis describes the Mercury in Scorpio perfectly. Only if you need to know, will you know. And even then, they might leave some things out just in case!

Mercury in Scorpio omits details to ensure they do not give away any information that can compromise them. Again, it is a trust thing. When no one person has all the pieces of information, the Mercury in Scorpio always has an out. This style frustrates people who collaborate or feel they need to know everything, and it can challenge someone managing a Mercury in Scorpio at work. The same can be said of parents of a Mercury in Scorpio. Anyone who has a vested interest in what the Mercury in Scorpio is doing will chafe at the shadowy communication. Mercury in Scorpio people enjoy building puzzles through their words, so one might have to spend time deciphering the true message being communicated, adding more barriers. Mercury in Scorpio do leave breadcrumbs, leading to discoverable information, but they will not make it easy.

Even in the best of times, their communication will feel a bit harsh. Their words can be like a scorpion's stinger, often coming off as strong and unyielding even if they are not trying to be or upset about anything. They will want to show their strength straight off the bat, which can work in some circumstances but not all. For example, business negotiations benefit from their fiery approach to communicating. When they compromise, the other side feels as if they have truly scored a point for their side without actually taking much away from the Mercury in Scorpio. Toning down this way of communicating is a Herculean task, but one worth tackling.

Moments do occur when a Scorpio in Mercury softens their style, but this is extraordinary linked to how they feel about the person or situation in the moment. How they feel about the receiver of the communication, where they feel their standing is with that person, whether or not they are comfortable in the situation dictates the engagement and the tone projected by the Mercury in Scorpio. If they are not feeling comfortable in the moment, expect one-word answers. Comfort, trust, and a sense of passion about a topic pushes the Mercury in Scorpio to communicate with openness, lightness, and fun. It is really a crapshoot; they can go either way from minute to minute. It really depends on the situation that they feel they're in.

Mercury in Scorpio is at their best when their passion erupts through their communication wall. When passion leads, their words will be flowery, heartfelt, authentic, and most importantly open. Mercury in Scorpio's body language plays a significant role in how they communicate. Scorpios in general communicate through their body, and this trait is heightened when Mercury is in Scorpio. Without saying a word, their facial expression or body language speaks to their mood and thoughts on a situation. They can chastise a person with a look that is stronger than any words they would say or write. Equally, a smile from a Mercury in Scorpio channels love and approval better than an epic poem. Gauging how a Mercury in Scorpio walks into a room can avert unwanted or unexpected confrontations.

Inspired Transformation

Elevated communication for a Mercury in Scorpio centers on increasing your level of trust in yourself and others. Trusting others with more information and letting them feel your passion will create a flow that benefits you and the others in your life.

1. Stop hiding information. Not everyone is out to get you, and the more you share the more you will receive in return. Earning trust is very valuable.
2. Take the edge off. When writing, read your words more than once before sharing them with others. Try to put yourself in their shoes and ask yourself how they would receive what you have written. When speaking, be aware your words have power to hurt, so take it slow so you can edit along the way.
3. Don't play favorites in your communication. Even if you are not excited about a situation or passionate about a person, try to speak as if you are, particularly at work. Being even-keeled ensures you can bring people on board with your way of thinking.
4. Remove barriers. Try not to make people jump through hoops to understand what it is you are trying to say. Being more direct helps you get where you want to go faster.
5. Be passionate. When you are, your communication skills naturally improve.

Sagittarius

Sagittarians are the world travellers of the Zodiac. Traveling, meeting new cultures, exploring remote locations, and planning unique adventures occupies a large part of the Sagittarian's world. Whether they are physically moving or scratching their itch via books or movies, they have an insatiable desire to see other places, not sit still, be on the move, and find new places or things to try.

This makes sense given Sagittarius is a Fire Sign with the internal element of air. That mix of fire and air infuses Sagittarians with bright, fun, big personalities, attracting attention because people feel their energy. Comfortable in the limelight, Sagittarians view the opportunity to be the center of attention to advance their opinions and wisdom for the betterment of the world, not necessarily themselves, as is more common to the other Fire Signs.

Voracious learners, Sagittarians rank high on the intelligence ladder. Like other Air Signs, topical variety reigns. However, Sagittarians will take the time to become more expert in one topic before moving on to the next. They pride themselves on being able to keep up with experts in a field even if they would not consider themselves one. For a Sagittarian, sharing what they have learned with others is more important than learning themselves. Having gifts for understanding what they learn, processing information very quickly, and communicating it directly, they make excellent teachers and pundits. They revel in recounting stories of their travels, what they have learned from other cultures, and their adventures, taking listeners on the journey with them.

Sagittarians are the most direct communicators of the Zodiac. They have no filter. We will learn more about this soon, but this is one of the Achilles' heels of a Sagittarian. They really just do not know how to say things with any awareness of how the receiver of the message might feel as a result.

Another challenge for the Sagittarian derives from a lack of desire to engage in any process. The world is built on process. Nothing created in this world arrives without a process. Sagittarians' fondness for engaging in the process is limited. They want to know or have decided what their desired outcome is, and they stick to it. In their mind, the way they see it is how it needs to be.

A helpful analogy illuminates this point. If a Sagittarian starts a new book, they read the end of the book first to discover the outcome and then go back and read the whole book to reveal how the outcome came to be. Once they know the outcome the journey feels more pleasurable. This focus on the outcome reveals the deep desire of Sagittarians to control. They literally try to manipulate every situation and scenario to advance themselves and those around them to the desired outcome. For example, envision a Sagittarian parent who wants their child to grow up to be a doctor. Deciding at the child's birth the actions they will take regarding the child's education, who their friends are, what their hobbies are, drive to that end. How the child feels about being a doctor becomes irrelevant to the parent. The Sagittarian parent has the vision for them and that is that.

The Sagittarian's control issues backfire most of the time. Short-term wins garner long-term losses. Deeper relationships bear the scars of the controlled plans set forth by the Sagittarian. Push back, avoidance, or flat out leaving occur as the Sagittarian tries to maintain the path to their envisioned end.

They truly believe they can control everything and are surprised when that is not the case, so disappointment and feeling let down by themselves and others creep into their lives. Frustration when others reject their bidding or when situations veer off their chosen path, takes over their lighthearted demeanor, starting a cycle of trying to control more as they lose control.

Trying to control everything results in another less obvious challenge for the Sagittarian. By trying to achieve one specific outcome, they leave a lot of potential gain on the table. For example, a Sagittarian entrepreneur wants investment in their company. They decide they want $1,000,000, and they are willing to give up 20 percent for that. That is the number, and they are sticking to it. In their search for investors, they might meet someone who is willing to invest $900,000 for 20 percent and introduce them to 50 potential customers who might increase their business tenfold. Because the terms do not meet the objective the Sagittarian wants, they reject it--even though the introductions to the customers might be more valuable in the long run than the initial investment. If the entrepreneur does not move the investor to their decided outcome, they will likely walk away. The controlling aspect of a Sagittarian holds them back from really receiving all the blessings they truly want.

Within any process, obstacles arise. Without an appreciation for the process, Sagittarians struggle to handle those road bumps, turning back or walking away--especially if they believe in an alternative route to their destination. The Sagittarian never imagines that road also might be fraught with road bumps as well because that is part of the process. Diving into the challenge or letting go of the exact outcome can be a remedy for the Sagittarian in this area.

Sagittarians enjoy relationships, but with all the fire and air in their constitution, they need to feel free to be who they are and to go where they want to go. Any committed relationship that feels as if it anchors them will not survive, so it is important to give the Sagittarius the room to move figuratively and literally. Sagittarians have been known to move often or have multiple homes. The controlling attribute of the Sagittarian plays a big impact in most of their close relationships, which is paradoxical because they absolutely do not want to be controlled. Those closest to the Sagittarians learn how to set their boundaries openly so the Sagittarian knows what to expect and to not take things too personally.

Financially, Sagittarians generate money, but they use it as fast as they earn it on their adventures. Any planning for the future originates in the desire to have the freedom they want. They love the good things in life, and they will spend to obtain them--regardless of the cost. The best careers for Sagittarians include teacher, mediator, writer, sociologist, anthropologist, journalist, and entrepreneur--anything where they can learn every day and share what they learned.

Mercury in Sagittarius

As mentioned previously, Sagittarian's style of communication is extraordinarily direct with a side of harshness. Their directness and lack of filter can be tough for people on the receiving end. If a Sagittarius wants to tell you something, good or bad, they're going to just flat-out tell you. They are not going to prepare you. They are not going to mince words. They are not going to be empathetic. They're just going to say it. For example, if you had your hair cut and they don't like it, they're going to tell you your hair looks ugly. No filter. No empathy. No regrets.

Times exist when directness is appropriate and appreciated, and the Mercury in Sagittarius can be the perfect person to navigate these moments. However, more times than not, the direct style has the opposite effect.

In any setting, whether business or personal, the direct Sagittarius style can, and does, hurt. The challenge for Mercury in Sagittarius is the typical Sagittarius directness is amplified tenfold because of the influence of Mercury, so the damage that can be done is intensified. Forethought and malice are not present, it is just the Mercury in Sagittarius sees their direct style as practical and useful. It cuts through and gets to the point, so they are often surprised by the response their communication provokes. Any recognition of the harm they might have caused will come after the fact and often after the person who was the recipient of the direct communication confronts them.

Mercury in Sagittarius are inquisitive. They drive to get to the bottom of anything and will do so by asking tons of questions. Sometimes the questions will be inflammatory to throw the receiver off, causing them to reveal more than they wanted. Most times, the questions will be pointed like the tip of an arrow.

Because Mercury in Sagittarius is well read, their communication reads like a book. Vivid descriptions color their communication like an artist paints a landscape. Their use of words will inspire the reader or listener to take a path of discovery themselves because a Mercury in Sagittarius activates curiosity and a love of exploration. They are simply fun to listen to and are super clever.

Dialogues with a Mercury in Sagittarius garner a load of benefit because they are engaged. They offer great advice, insight, and support.

Their controlling Sagittarius instinct shows up in their communications as well. It is called spin. They will lead you only where they want you to go, providing only the information they think relevant to drag you to the response they want you to have. Recognize they will manipulate any communication to serve their purpose. Keeping information out of their communication is not deceitful in their minds, it is a way to ensure the outcome, so it feels perfectly reasonable to them even if not to anybody else. When you are receiving information from a Sagittarius, you might want to do some research of your own only to ensure you are getting the whole picture and that you have the information you need to act in the way you want to act.

Sagittarians will manipulate others into the conversations as well. They want to build consensus, but they want to control how individuals arrive at the same place so they will take the time to have one-on-one conversations until they are satisfied that everyone is on the same playing field. Again, manipulation is part of the game for them, so they keep control.

Inspired Transformation

The message for the Mercury in Sagittarius is practice compassion, empathy, and taking a beat before you speak. Your words have power, and more of them will be received if you think before you talk.

1. Filter your words. The direct approach does not always garner your desired response.
2. Stop the spin. Sharing more information might produce more collaboration and better results than you might imagine.
3. Let go of how and when your objectives will be met. Allowing others to participate in the conversation and persuade you can lead can take you places you never imagined.
4. Connect to your heart. When you communicate emotion and vulnerability, you open up others to embrace your messages.
5. Expand your audience. Your words impact people, and the more you can impact in a positive way, the better. Write a book, create a podcast, or find other ways to share your wisdom with a broader audience.

Capricorn

Capricorns are recognized as the hardest working sign of the Zodiac. They equate hard work with success. If they are working hard, they are successful, no matter how much money they earn. In fact, they can work hard on playing as well! Work eases their minds, and it can be an emotional retreat. Capricorns leave the office last and then come back in before anyone else the next morning. Reliability is their middle name. They meet deadlines, and they ensure their work is exceptional, accurate, and double-checked. When a task must be done, a Capricorn is the best person to complete it.

Capricorn is an Earth Sign with an internal water element. Methodical in their approach to everything, a Capricorn takes no shortcuts at all. Every step a Capricorn takes is thought through and precise. A good analogy arises from the animal representing the sign of Capricorn, the goat. Like a mountain goat going up the side of a mountain, each step counts to reach the top and also for their survival. A goat steps very carefully, safeguarding them from plunging to their death. Likewise, the Capricorn maintains their balance and focus to get the job done. Rushing a Capricorn produces little effect on the speed at which they will complete their work. They do it at the speed that works for them.

Manifesting matters to a Capricorn. They avoid undertaking anything they feel they might struggle to finish and finish well. If they say they are going to do something, they will keep moving until they meet their objective. Persistence is a hallmark feature of the Capricorn nature. They do not let go of things very easily, causing a loss of vision of why they started that something in the first place. They lose sight of the bigger picture. Going back to the analogy of a goat going up a mountain, they are so focused on every step they forget about the destination they are seeking. However, from a tactical execution and getting things done standpoint, there isn't anybody better to go to than a Capricorn.

Materialism powers the Capricorn's engine. The things they have and the money they earn validates them and provides a perceived feeling of respect. Things indicate something about them without them having to say anything. Materialism walks hand in hand with working hard because the harder they feel they work, the more money they earn, the more things they can buy, the more people respect them, and the better they feel about themselves. It is a continuous cycle connected to achievement.

Unfortunately, this cycle is misaligned with a Capricorn's true purpose. The internal water aspect points to a deep well of intuition and emotion that would provide a much greater payoff for the Capricorn than what hard work offers. The extent of their intuitive nature is far greater than that of a Water Sign because of the difficulty for them to access it as they run their lives by the motto, "Seeing is believing," instead of, "Believing is seeing."

When Capricorns release themselves from the attachment to the material and physical worlds, they can open a significant channel to their intuition, the voice inside of them that can guide them and others if they choose more fruitful paths than focusing on the material world allows. Another benefit of letting go of putting the material world in front of everything else, is the Capricorn gains back other more important aspects of life, including their relationships with others and critically themselves. Striving for all things physical and using that as validation creates a non-sustainable, false economy where loneliness and bitterness become the currency.

Capricorns exhibit high motivation to achieve when there is a tangible reward attached to the outcome, which can be good in certain circumstances. The bigger the perceived or real payoff, the more Capricorn will work to achieve their goal. This drives them up the corporate ladder--or any ladder for that matter! If you ever want to motivate a Capricorn child to finish their homework or to do something they do not want to do try offering them money, more time on their video games or time with their friends. You will see them jump to comply with your request. On the other hand, being motivated by material rewards puts barriers up between them and the things that truly count like relationships.

Their approach to their tasks is straight forward, following the rules, taking their time, and going in what they consider the "right way" sticking to that path no matter what, expecting the same from others. Multitasking does not come easily to a Capricorn; they tackle one task at a time. As a result, they kind of isolate themselves and put themselves in a position where they take on the burden of everything, not asking for assistance when they need it. They do not seek advice, they just go and do and go and do, go and do. This habit gives off the vibe to others that they are not team players, which on a certain level is true. They trust themselves more than they trust anyone else, and they rely on themselves more than they do others to reach their goals because they believe the reward will be better if they show they can achieve it alone.

Their relationship with others challenges the Capricorn crowd. Somewhat aloof and typically introverted, alone time ranks as a favorite pastime. They prefer to find a nice corner and tick boxes on their to-do lists. They can act a little standoffish at first glance and take a slow, steady approach to developing relationships whether personal or professional. They are choosy about who swirls in their inner circle, frankly they want to know how a person might impact them on their journey to achieving their goals.

Loyalty to their small network of friends shines through as does their commitment. Once you are in with a Capricorn, you are in. Not known for light and breezy, chit-chat the idea of just socializing bristles them. One could have a Capricorn friend who they have not spoken to for two or three years and the Capricorn might call them one of their best friends!

They take their time developing relationships, bringing somebody into their fold allowing them to see who they truly are and offering up their valuable achievement time to just hang out. For romantic relationships, once they dive in and feel they found the one, they commit. There would have to be a seismic event to move them off a relationship once they committed. Capricorns are not known for extramarital affairs or even multiple marriages. They would rather be stable.

Financially, the Capricorn is one of the strongest money generators, earners, and savers of the whole Zodiac. They succeed financially simply because they are hard workers. They won't take huge risks like an entrepreneur would or play the stock market like it is Vegas. They work hard for what they earn, and they prefer it that way. They tend to be frugal with what they earn—but not stingy. For example, they will spend a good bit of time researching the type of car they want to buy, and when they find it and love it, they will keep it for years and years. Their thought is, *Why buy a new car if I love this one, it works, there is still value, and I don't have to spend money on a new car payment?* They love eking the value out of everything they own.

Generosity lurks just under a Capricorn's skin and emerges when they see a clear purpose and a solid method attached to how their money will be used. They are excellent investors because of their methodical approach and their ease with hanging in there, not being affected by ups and downs. They do not need a quick win.

They understand that things take time. They understand the process. They know that if they just push through or hold their money in a certain stock it is going to have a payoff because they have done their research.

Mercury in Capricorn

People with Mercury in Capricorn amplify the Capricorn energy in they will be hyper methodical. If they are going to explain something, they are going to explain it step by step, by step, by step. They will not shortcut their communications. And if you try to make them, their reaction will be negative. Their thinking means something to them, and they want to have the opportunity to show that thinking to others. If a Capricorn is asked to write a report on any given topic, the report will exhibit logic and assist in reaching the objective. Whatever the objective of the report is, the length will be substantial, not a quick recap.

Mercury in Capricorn finds no need to talk a lot. If asked a question, they will answer what they need to answer. They'll tell you what they need to tell you, and that is it. They are not hiding anything, but unlike in their written form, they will be short and sweet about it. Their language lacks a flowery, emotional quality, rather taking a straightforward tone. Although that depth of internal water energy might allow some emotions to bubble up, they will try and squash them. One might feel the struggle as they listen to them because the conflict between being deeply emotional and very stable, grounded, and logical is real.

Mercury in Capricorn is a little bit icy and robotic in their communication. Their tone and inflection are almost monotone with little fluctuation. They are not looking to draw you in; they are all about the facts, ma'am! They desire to receive more facts or to convey the facts, because that's really what's important to them. If one is in a relationship with a Mercury in Capricorn person, and they desire emotions they are not going to go there. They will not engage. Engaging in emotional conversations is completely out of their comfort zone.

Highly rated in business communications, Mercury in Capricorn write exactly what is needed, how it's needed, and make sure it's steeped in facts. Mistakes are uncommon, and the backup research is solid and reliable. Delivering hard messages or negative news does not rattle them because they focus on the facts and leave the emotions to the side.

Mercury in Capricorn people are not great entrepreneurs because taking risks repels them, but they are solid executives and middle managers in almost any field they choose because they will stick to their work and become an expert in the field.

Inspired Thoughts

The overall message for Mercury in Capricorn people to improve their communication skills centers on allowing their emotion to shine through their communication, instead of hanging on to the objective of their communication. Your communications will be better received and more impactful when others feel you.

1. Let loose. Allow your voice and words drip with the emotion you are feeling. That really helps you smash the wall and activate more.
2. Go with the flow. Not everything has to be meticulous and step-by-step. While people do like to know what is required, they also like to show their skills, which in the end assists you more in achieving your objectives.
3. Dialogue more. Get out with others and engage in conversation that has little purpose other than to get to know others. Speak, share, and put yourself out there more. Sometimes it is good to communicate just for the sake of communicating. There doesn't have to be a win or goal in it for you. If you want to just call someone to say hello, just do it.
4. Lighten up. Add a little flare to your communication. Do some creative writing to practice writing for the sake of sharing a fun story, not for any other reason.
5. Collaborate more. Solitary working does not equal better working. Ask for help and support and let others bring their great ideas to the table.

Aquarius

If you want to start a revolution, find an Aquarian to lead the way. The sign of Aquarius is the rebel of the Zodiac and the world. Rules are meant to be broken, and disruption for the sake of progress enlivens an Aquarian. Change rocks, progress breathes life into the world, and throwing out the old to build something new drives the Aquarian sensibility and sense of action. Figuring out how to do things better is their lifeblood.

Aquarius is an Air Sign, sporting the internal element of fire. They carry a "burn it down to build it up" vibe in all they do. Aquarians start worldwide movements, especially in times of oppression or extreme challenges. They stand at the front lines and drive forward the changes that in their opinions will change the whole world. They expertly coalesce people behind their movement, raising awareness, money, and sometimes temperatures along the way. They truly want to help, and their desire to do so originates from a very authentic internal place. They want to change the world for the better, never just for themselves or for recognition.

My description might sound as if they only start movements on a global scale, but Aquarians will take the lead on small causes as well. They will aim to make an impact any place they believe they can.

Aquarians ooze intelligence, logically mapping out a path for arriving where they want to go. They soar at 30,000 feet, focusing on a big-picture view of the world. Strategy is their jam, and they find doing to be harder than leading others to do what they need. Hard to pin down, they move fluidly from one task to the next in their revolution, multi-thinking, yet at the same time staying focused on pushing their change the world agenda forward. Their internal fire energy provides an unusual focus for the Air Sign because it fans their passion. Passion is their anchor, and without it, they would struggle to manifest their vision of change.

Aquarians want to get things done. They absolutely want to see the effects of the energy they release into the world. Masters at convincing others that what they are selling is the right thing, even the best thing for them and the world, they drag people into metaphorical battle. Even with skeptics among the crowd, the way an Aquarian presents their case, showing how what they are talking about is logically going to change the world is intoxicating. It's also convincing and perceived as doable, so people will jump on board and say, "Okay, I want to do that."

All this energy is great, and Aquarians' desire to change the world is important, but it comes with a challenge. Because their passion drives them and their lens is strategic leaning on the bigger picture, they often forget to engage with people one-on-one or they step on people to get to where they want, instead of bringing them along throughout the process. They feel their mission and cause are bigger than the people they are fighting for, so accomplishing the mission becomes more important than the people themselves. They do what they do for the sake of people, yet if someone blocks their road, they opt to move right past them. Aquarius struggles with this paradox. An Aquarius can walk into a room and not even say hello to the person who they are there to help because they are on another planet, planning what they need to do. They are literally in space, and that one-on-one interaction feels less important than saving the world.

Their push beyond the individuals takes much away from their interpersonal relationships. They want to achieve what they want, in the way they want to achieve it, without regard for what their achievement might do to other people along the way. They love humanity, but human beings are a different story because human beings individually have unique needs, and their vision might not work for everybody, which forces them to question their mission. That is too much for them to take.

Aquarians' rebellious nature poses challenges in other areas of their lives as well. Aquarians look to push the envelope in every way, putting opportunities like their jobs at risk. When they see something they disagree with, they do not have a problem stating their mind because they feel saying something is for the greater good. However, maybe their boss does not agree or does not want to hear their argument. Instead of just getting on with their work, it is common for an Aquarian to rebel because they feel their purpose is to right the wrongs. But if they push it, they could lose their job.

Aquarians are super creative, activating their mind to think about all the new ways to evolve any process to the next level. For example, how do you change a governmental system and make it better? How do you improve a military system? They're always thinking about more ways to change the status quo and the standard operating procedures. However, it is difficult for them to wait around to see if what they planted actually works. They have already moved on both mentally and physically. They are so confident in their vision and plan once it is implemented that they start to think about what they want to conquer next.

Regarding relationships, Aquarians struggle with long-term, committed relationships mainly because of their lack of connection on a one-on-one level. At the start, the connection will be great, but when it gets deeper and expectations increase, they find ways to move on to the next one. It is not odd for an Aquarian to have multiple relationships, as they never really settled down. Aquarians have lots of friends, but they keep the relationships with them at the surface level. Keep it light, airy, simple. If a person gets too needy, that is a sure way to send an Aquarian packing the other direction. And if a person in a relationship with an Aquarian seeks empathy or an emotional, lovey dovey connection, they will be disappointed. Aquarians are very much in-their-head thinkers, and emotions do not have a place in their cause-driven world.

Relationships with Aquarians can be somewhat confusing. It isn't that they don't love, but they need their space. They need to be able effortlessly go off on their quests and save the world. If a person is unable to handle that lifestyle choice, the Aquarian will just move on with no emotion tied to it.

Aquarian careers require innovation, caused-based values, and variety to keep them motivated. They must believe their job aligns with their need for higher purpose. Politics, law, technology, and nonprofits all capture the interest of Aquarians, and they are good at them. Strategy, complex communication, and desire highlight the skill section of the resume. Whatever career they are in, they will find the cause d'jour in it. If they're scientists, they're going to be the researchers answering the biggest questions in science. If they are accountants, they are going to be transforming accountancy practices. Whatever it is, they're going to find the cause in it, and they are going to wrap themselves up in that.

Money comes and goes in the world of the Aquarian. They have the talent to make money, but they also like to fund their causes. But even more so, they are not compelled to earn a lot of money because they live simply. Especially if they're saving the world, they want to live comfortably enough and finance their causes, whatever that is. Money is not their primary attachment. Equally, they probably won't be saving a lot of money along the way because they will be investing in their causes or in the things that align with their passions.

Mercury in Aquarius

Mercury in Aquarius style consists of quick bursts of focused communication that includes direction they expect you to absorb and execute because they are leading the way, and they just need you to follow. Embellished words are not the Mercury in Aquarius way, but they will be inspiring in a simple way. Their words are going to be brief. They will put loads of energy into their words so they will be felt and heard in their communication. This is their gift and how they build their army. The way they build consensus is to prove why what they want to do is going to be better than what exists today. They draw in others by making them feel they are on their side, thinking about their best interest, which for the most part is true. However, part of it is also for the sake of building the army to serve their objective. They want to make sure their cause is moving forward, and they will do what they have to--even if it is not for the benefit of everyone individually. There might be an agenda. With Mercury in Aquarius, it is prudent to learn more about what the agenda is and how everyone lining up behind them benefits.

A Mercury in Aquarius person speaks in commanding phrases, such as "Get the job done," "I need this to happen," "I need you to be on my side," and "I need you to have my back." They are passionate and concise. Deep emotion, sympathy, and empathy are nowhere to be found in communications from a Mercury in Aquarius. Let's do it this way. Let's do it this way. Do it fast and do it, do it the way I'm telling you.

In direct confrontation with Mercury in Aquarius, one will be out-thought and out- logic'd. You will not get a word in edgewise because they will circle you down the drain with their logic until you give up. Debating with Mercury in Aquarius can be very, very difficult. It is not a fun thing to do.

On the other hand, when Mercury in Aquarius is relaxed and when not leading the charge, you will find they have a wonderful sense of humor. They are light and airy, so their communication can be creative and funny. Even though they can be commanding, they are not heavy. They don't want to be the downer in the room because they want people to be on their side, and persuasion cannot be hard to take in. They know how to match their communication to effectively open up people to their message.

Inspired Transformation

The number one message for the Mercury in Aquarius revolves around connecting one-on-one with the recipient of their communications. Remember the little guy; you cannot make it without them. They need love and understanding as well as persuasion and direction.

1. Have a heart. Think about others when you're speaking, being authentic and honest. Convey the care you have for the world at large to them.

2. Drop the cause. Not everything has to change the world. Not every communication needs to be a rallying cry. Reach out to someone and say hello for no reason.
3. Get your head out of the clouds. Just because you can see the bigger picture does not mean everyone can. Provide more details so others know what you need and also why you need it. You might be able to recruit more people to be long-term supporters of your cause.
4. Logic does not always win out. Try to understand that just because you can outthink someone doesn't mean you should. Winning is not the be-all end-all, so allow people to disagree with you and share their side of the story. Sometimes conflicts need to have emotions come out for things to advance.
5. Embellish! Take more time with your communication. Short and sweet can be confusing for the receiver. The more you share, the more you can persuade people to see the value in your cause.

Pisces

Pisces is the last and most spiritually driven sign of the Zodiac. As the last sign, they are said to encompass a little piece of all the other signs, meaning they have an innate ability to connect deeply with all people. Unbelievably sensitive to the world around them, empathy marks the cornerstone of their personality. They actually feel people around them in a significant way. They feel everybody's pain, happiness, anger, and disappointment. They sense when a person's emotional equilibrium is off--even if they have never met them before. In some ways, they are so empathetic they almost lose themselves in others' pain.

A Pisces' empathetic nature and connection to emotions elevates them to the role of go-to person when a situation requires understanding, support, and unconditional love. They will do whatever they can to ease pain. They will take on the burden of other people's pain often to their own detriment, which is where the downside of that kind of deep empathy lives.

Pisces is a Water Sign with the internal energy of air. Like the other Water Signs, Pisces own a heightened level of intuition, but the internal air adds an angle of intelligence where they not only feel but they also know. They contain a solid sense of what the entire journey of humanity is and where it will end, so they move through life with an uncanny sense that everything is always going to be okay. They do not need to worry about the material world, just the people in it. The idea of death holds no power over them.

Money ebbs and flows for Pisces. They keenly understand that if it is a period where money is ebbing, just give it some time and it will flow again, and money matters little in humanity's big picture.

While not always openly on display, Pisces possess psychic abilities.

Pisces are non-linear thinkers, leaving no room for logic. Like a fish moving through the water going this way and that with no set direction to get to where they want to go, the Pisces mind processes information and conveys information in an abstract manner. They might start at point A, but then they will skip to point L and return to point B before they find their way to point Z, their final destination. They ponder life in very unexpected ways because of their meandering thoughts and keen emotions. Creativity abounds, and unique expressions of their inner thoughts arises.

However, the Pisces requires the latitude to go through this seemingly confusing process. A rushed Pisces freezes, unable to make a clear decision, so those around them are wise to give a wide berth while they process. The depth of their emotions and ability to go with the flow imbues them with creativity that expands from the creative arts, to writing to creative business propositions.

Despite their unique perspective and creative thinking, Pisces struggle to manifest because they tend to move where the tide takes them, going in circles and getting caught in a rut instead of driving themselves to their objective. They possess an attitude that they will get to their objective when they get there, and in the meantime, whatever happens, happens. They do not feel like they need to or want to be in control. They feel happiest when they allow the universe to guide them.

Pisceans are typically low on desire, but thanks to their internal air element, they do have an appetite for success--even if their internal drive takes some time to rev up the engine. The level in life they are at is usually the place where they want to be. They move at their own pace in their own way, which can be challenging for people who want them to get things done, especially in their careers.

When confronted with anything uncomfortable, Pisceans bury their heads in the sand. They are cosmic ostriches. If a situation makes them uncomfortable, they avoid it at all costs. They will just ignore it until the circumstances make it impossible for them to continue to avoid. And even then, they will try to put their head in the sand again because they feel so overwhelmed. Confrontation is extremely difficult for a Piscean, primarily because they are so connected and empathetic to other people that they don't want to rock boats. They feel the pain of rocking the boat themselves, so confrontation acts almost like a self-inflicted wound. That is why the easier road for them is to ignore rather than dive in to try to find a solution.

On top of this, they have the instinctive view that the universe is going to fix the challenge anyway, so why get their hands dirty along the way. They ask themselves, "Why do I need to do it? Nothing I can do is going to change the outcome." So back goes their head into the sand, exacerbating the troubles. Whether they are aware of it or not, it is their coping mechanism, and they end up holding the bag a lot for their own mistakes.

Another coping mechanism to drown out the intense internal nd empathetic feeling they have is addiction. Whether drugs, alcohol, food, television, or shopping, their addictions help them to avoid things that bring them discomfort. They reach for anything to take them out of the pain that they don't want to feel. And unfortunately, because they feel so many other people's pain as well, it can make it too overwhelming for them, and they don't even know why. Their addiction might come in spite of their life seeming to be perfectly wonderful. Happiness around them does not always ease the pain they seek to dull. The battle to overcome addiction is difficult because their addiction soothes them, and they want to be soothed.

Pisceans excel in relationships because they are naturally loving and compassionate. Commitment comes easy, but sometimes they can be committed to someone unhealthy for them. Co-dependency is common in Piscean relationships because they authentically feel the pain of their partner and want to ease the pain for them both, so they take on a lot of the burden for the relationship.

Homebodies and slightly introverted, Pisceans would rather spend time with close friends and family than venture out, exposing themselves to many people's energy. They enjoy being self-reflective and using their emotions creatively, so they will never mind staying home and creating space for themselves to heal. They often practice more than one spiritual path because spirituality feels like home.

Pisces are soft people, meaning hard edges cannot be found. In relationships, they are very understanding. They will take the time to hear what people have to say, ensuring they allow the person to be themselves, allowing them to talk, vent, scream, and do whatever they need to feel better. They won't let people down.

Financially, Pisceans are good channels for money because they do not get too attached to money. It seems to flow. Their intuitive nature aids them in building profitable investment portfolios. They sense when it is the right time to buy or sell, whether a company is on the right track, or whether the market is going up or down. They will do the research to back up their instinct, but they just know what they know. They also are very adept at letting go and asking the universe to guide them, looking for signs along the way. They manage money very well--unless they fall into an addiction that syphons the money away from them. They know from the bottom of their soul that money is an energetic tool as long as they do not stay too attached to it. All things being equal, they will have more than what they need. This attitude promotes generosity and a sharing disposition.

Pisceans excel in people-centric careers. Sales, social work, therapy, medicine, education, and nonprofit organizations focused on supporting people directly tend to work with the Pisces mindset.

Mercury in Pisces

The Mercury in Pisces communication style is indirect and soft. They will not directly come out and say what they think. They edit their words as they are speaking and will be deferential, almost apologizing for what they are about to say before they say it. They can be verbose because it takes them time to explain how they are starting at point A, going all the way to point L, then back again. It won't make sense to most people, so explanation is required in their communication.

They are notorious for interrupting their own thought process out loud as they figure out what they want to say. They will be talking and then suddenly, they jump to another adjacent topic that might have relevance to what they were saying or not. The receiver might not understand the jump, but if they have patience, the Mercury in Pisces will eventually bring it home. Their communications are unintentionally convoluted--like parallel conversations are happening all at once and they are connecting the dots in their head, but it is not always easy for somebody else to understand right away.

Mercury in Pisces communicates with their emotions on their sleeve and their face. They cannot hide how they feel, whether they are speaking in person with somebody or communicating in writing. People feel their emotions in what they do, what they say, and how they say it. This attribute carries a lot of benefits, inspiring people to align with them because the Mercury in Pisces is emotionally connected and passionate to their topic. They will reveal their vulnerability in their communications, attracting help and support from others.

Their communications reference their experiences, not from an ego standpoint but rather to exhibit they are just like the recipient of their communication, putting them at ease and making them feel a kinship that builds trust. If a Mercury in Pisces has specific knowledge about the person they are speaking to, they will find affinity through that connection, with their words and stories generating a bond that may result in mutually beneficial outcomes. Mercury in Pisces understands the power of their intuitive, empathetic nature and will use that to their advantage.

Mercury in Pisces tops the charts when it comes to delivering a difficult message. The message will be padded with an abundance of deeply felt emotional content to soften the blow. For example, if the Mercury in Pisces must fire an employee, they will find the words to help the person feel like being fired is the best thing for them at that moment.

When communicating, Mercury in Pisces take on a lot on themselves, taking the blame or sharing the praise for something they did. For example, imagine an email needs to go to an employee who made a mistake, losing money for the company reprimanding them and admonishing them to not make that same mistake again. The Mercury in Pisces will reprimand the employee but will also be a mea culpa, taking joint responsibility for the mistake. They will express the mea culpa sympathetically, wanting to guarantee the employee does not take the brunt of the blame and feel bad about the situation.

Their creative nature shines through in their communication, artistically crafting words and sentences that help the recipient visualize the journey they are taking them on. Their communications can be very funny and playful, evocative, or placating, clever, and thoughtful. One would struggle to find communications from Mercury in Pisces boring, but one must hang in there with them to get to the "punchline," which can cause them to lose their audience.

An area for growth is to learn to be more concise and straight with their communications and know that direct does not necessarily mean hurtful.

Inspired Transformation

The transformational theme for Mercury in Pisces is learning how to balance their incredible empathy with direct communication, not allowing their concern for how everyone feels cloud their ability to make their necessary points. Not every situation requires a soft approach.

1. Be direct. Work on not beating around the bush and say what needs to be said. Practice by putting time limits on yourself when writing.
2. Stop equivocating and put your needs before others' needs. Start your communication with what you want, leaving out the apologies.
3. Shorten the explanation path. There is a time to show your work, and there is a time to give an answer without explanation. Work on using your words more efficiently.

4. Close the loop. Don't leave things open-ended. Try to bring things to a conclusion by helping people understand what the most important point is.
5. Buck up! Your emotions are amazing, but they don't always need to be on display. It is not about hiding them, rather it is about bringing them out at the best time, not every time.

Acknowledgments

I would like to acknowledge Jennifer Bright of Bright Communications for helping me believe being an author was well within my reach and even closer than I thought. Thank you for your belief, support, and your amazing energy along the way.

About the Author

Wendy Rosenthal, Chief Pathfinder is a mom, a wife, an avid sports fan, a podcaster, lecturer, a person who has been on a spiritual path for 25 years, a good friend who loves to help people.

For the last 25 years Wendy has been advising businesses, large and small around the world on how to take an idea and turn it into something that can come to life, all the while supporting their brand and financial objectives. From theme parks in Abu Dhabi to non-profits in Los Angeles, she has seen a lot projects fly and others never get off the ground. She learned from the best in many industries and has seen people, titans of industry, make mistakes...all of which made their projects better in the long run.

Along the way, Wendy realized the best part of her consulting work was being able to work one to one with people in the teams she supported, helping them play their part in the overall team.

This inspired her to shift her consulting focus using her gift of taking a lot of information in and distilling it to clear a pathway for action that helps individuals move their ideas to creation, to jump over all their own internal and external hurdles with clarity and ease.

Ultimately, her goal is always to empower her clients to discover the answers that are inside them already and be the support they need to achieve their next greatness whatever that may be.

Wendy lives in Austin, Texas, with her husband, Mike; son, David; and dog, Sunnie.

www.ingramcontent.com/pod-product-compliance
Lightning Source LLC
Chambersburg PA
CBHW071205120626
46546CB00006B/2432